Bonanza Victorian

"There is no more conclusive testimony of the state of civilization of a people, than that to be found in their Architecture."

—Samuel Sloan, October 1868

BONANZA VICTORIAN

Architecture and Society
in Colorado Mining Towns

C. Eric Stoehr

UNIVERSITY OF NEW MEXICO PRESS

Albuquerque

Designed by Dan Stouffer and Barbara Hoon

To Gail, my wife, researcher, traveling companion, note taker, photograph printer, adviser, and critic, whose love for Colorado inspired the writing of this book, and whose continuous support, encouragement, and enthusiasm provided the incentive without which this work would have greatly suffered

Contents

Illustrations

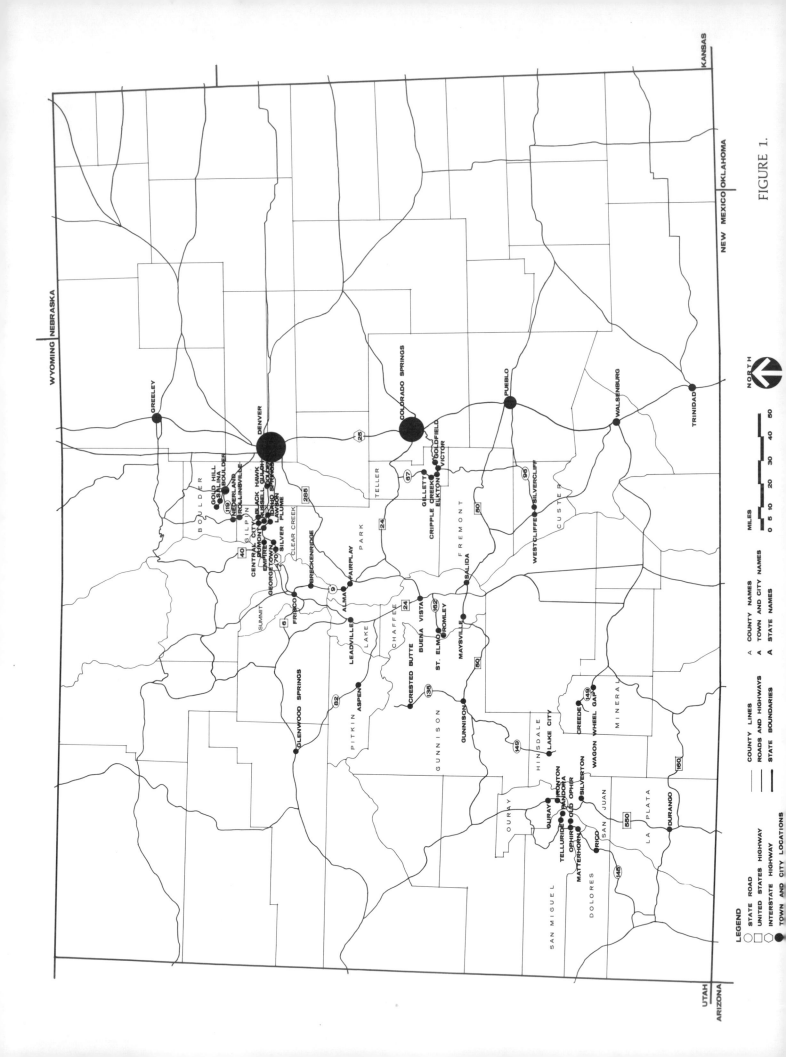

FIGURE 1.

Introduction

This book was written to provide a record of the unique and vanishing architectural forms of nineteenth-century Colorado mining towns. I gathered information for it in historical societies and libraries in Colorado and other states, and between September 1973 and December 1974 I visited over forty towns, to study and photograph them. All the photographs in the book are my own work. I have purposely avoided using old pictures from Colorado archives, as my intent is to show what remains of the towns now—what can be seen by the present-day visitor. The locations of the communities discussed here are shown on the map on page xii (fig. 1).

Architectural studies of earlier societies are often difficult, for in most cases other, later cultures have grown over them. The mining towns of Colorado, however, have been preserved, for the most part, by geographic and economic isolation. As communities ceased to be economically worthwhile, miners abandoned the towns. The remaining inhabitants lived and worked in existing structures; relatively few new buildings were constructed after the end of the great gold and silver booms at the turn of the century. As a result, we are able to look into another era and observe the structure of this unique mining society through its buildings.

All Colorado mining communities evolved through one or more of the following three phases: settlement phase, camp phase, and town phase. Most of the communities that are still intact reached the mining town phase of development. They offer the most representative sampling of the mining community architecture of Colorado and hence a better insight into the society. Since they have progressed through the earlier phases of settlement and camp, remains of all three stages can be found in almost every town today. Most of the communities examined here represent this phase of development, where the best remains can be found.

Many of the towns, which have stood for such a long time without significant change, are now being transformed in various ways. The natural deterioration of wood buildings and their vulnerability to fire have been constant factors in the disappearance of old towns. In addition, increasing vandalism and new booms in land development, such as the creation of ski areas and other recreational facilities, are contributing to the metamorphosis. Soon such transformation will make many of the original towns unrecognizable.

This study, for purposes of clarity, has been divided into two parts. Part I summarizes Colorado mining history and town planning. My account of this history, purposely brief, is only intended to provide the reader with background for the material that follows. The planning section is as complete as I deemed necessary for the understanding of the architecture. This book is not intended to be a study of town planning, but rather an investigation of the town architecture. Part II analyzes the building types that make up the mining community. These have been divided into the general categories of residential, commercial, institutional, and industrial. A general discussion of the influencing architectural styles has been included to prepare the reader for the analysis to follow.

I wish to thank Dr. Bainbridge Bunting and Edith Cherry of the School of Architecture and Planning of the University of New Mexico and Dr. Duane A. Smith of the Department of History of Fort Lewis College, Durango, Colorado, for their support and assistance in this project. I also would like to express my gratitude to Dr. Richard Ellis of the Department of History of the University of New Mexico and Muriel Sibell Wolle of Boulder, Colorado for their helpful suggestions. In addition, I wish to acknowledge the help given me by the librarians of the University of New Mexico and the University of Colorado; the Colorado Historical Society; the Missouri Historical Society; the historical societies of many of the mining communities; various museum staffs; citizens of the towns; and last but not least, the Victorians, who made this effort possible.

PART I

History and Town Planning

"A nation that forgets its past has no future."
—Winston Churchill

1
Colorado Mining History

Among the thousands who took Horace Greeley's advice to "go West, young man" were the vigorous young founders of Colorado. Apart from traders, freighters, trappers, Indian agents, explorers, soldiers, forty-niners, Spaniards, Mexicans, Mormons, and some travelers and sportsmen, few white men had ventured far west of the Missouri River prior to the Russell prospecting party of Georgia, which reached the Pikes Peak country in 1858 and prospected with moderate success on the tributaries of the Platte River, east of the base of the Rocky Mountains. The reports of gold strikes, mostly exaggerated, spread like wildfire in the states, and thousands prepared to visit the area the following spring. This was the year after the great financial crash of 1857, and men were ready for almost any venture that promised to better their fortune. The area known as the Pikes Peak gold region held out such a promise. The pioneers of the fall of 1858 founded the towns of Auraria, Denver, Boulder, Fountain City, and one or two minor settlements.

Hundreds of log cabins were built in the new towns to accommodate the builders and to sell or rent to the men who were sure to come in the spring. The spring and summer of 1859 brought a stampede westward equaled only by the California gold rush. "Gold," as a nineteenth-century writer said, "had created a fever and enthusiasm that no distance nor hardship could repress, no danger or difficulty dispel."[1] Over the six hundred miles of Kansas dust and solitude passed an almost continuous stream of humanity, traveling at an average rate of twenty miles a day. With "Pikes Peak or Bust" painted on the covers of their prairie schooners, many set forth with little conception of the distance to be covered or the supplies needed, and great suffering resulted. Many of the pioneers who settled Colorado were men of outstanding character and training; they came from the East, West, and South. About one hundred thousand men, mostly young, with no family obligations and no fear of hardship, made this migration in 1859. Nearly fifty thousand made it to Denver, of whom twenty-five thousand remained or went on to the mountains to seek their fortune. Farmers, speculators, merchants, mechanics, gamblers, doctors, lawyers, politicians, and wanderers from foreign lands, both cultured and illiterate, came to the new land of gold. Although many were able to adapt to the wilderness, large numbers became discouraged and went back home. Most of these gold seekers knew nothing about mining and the wild rush for wealth.

In the spring of 1859 the pioneers began to explore the foothills and mountains west of Denver. Placer mining was taking place on the streams where they left the mountains. Although some minor gold discoveries had been made earlier in the season, the most important find was that of John H. Gregory near Mountain City, between the present sites of Central City and Black Hawk. The first extensive deposit unearthed in Colorado, Gregory's discovery assured the gold hunters that they would find other valuable deposits. In addition, George A. Jackson had just discovered the richest placer deposits yet at the present site of Idaho Springs, and a third important discovery was made at Gold Hill in Boulder County. When word reached Denver that large amounts of gold existed less than forty miles away, a stampede resulted. Thousands of men soon camped in the area and rich deposits and veins were discovered in great numbers. Tent and pine-bough-shelter settlements blanketed the hills. Within a short time, Central City, with its stores, saloons, gambling houses, hotels, and express and printing offices, was an established town.

Mining districts needed their own laws, as these settlements were outside the jurisdiction of any state and remote in the territories within which they were located. Plains, mountains, and desert separated them from the rest of the country. All questions that arose were decided by majority vote at open-air meetings.

By the end of May the valleys and streams of newly established Clear Creek, Gilpin, and Boulder counties were alive with men. Cabins were erected and sluice boxes constructed for washing the gold from the pay dirt.

Later in the summer of 1859, as the localities that had been settled earlier became overpopulated, prospecting parties began to move out in search of other fields. Soon the camps of Hamilton, Tarryall, Jefferson City, and Fairplay evolved. In Clear Creek County, Idaho Springs was the leading town; in Gilpin County, Black Hawk, Mountain City, Central City, Missouri City, and Nevadaville were clustered together in the vicinity of the Gregory lode.

Early supply trains contained not only stocks of general merchandise, food, and mining tools, but sawmills and printing presses as well. The sawmills were soon turning out lumber for finishing the buildings that replaced crude log and tent structures. With the printing presses came the *Rocky Mountain News* and the *Cherry Creek Pioneer* in April 1859. In the spring of 1859 the Leavenworth and Pikes Peak Express Company established a six-day stage line over the six hundred miles between the Missouri River and the Rocky Mountains.

Although the vast majority of gold seekers came not to found new homes but to gather a fortune and return to their old homes to enjoy it, some decided that their futures lay in the West. While many traveled east during the winter of 1859–60, planning to return the following spring with their families, about ten thousand persons, mostly men, spent the winter in the new territory.

In 1860, mining continued vigorously as newcomers, five thousand a week at the peak, arrived from the East, and many new sections were explored. Most of the important early discoveries were made by men who had mined previously in Georgia or in California.

As the main point of arrival and departure for nearly all who came, Denver grew rapidly in 1860. Brick buildings were erected, and large business houses were established, including three banks. The June 6, 1860 edition of the *Rocky Mountain News* described Denver as follows:

> Our city—commenced in the winter of 58–59—in the spring of 1859 containing a motley collection of three hundred log huts covered with mud, and on the first of July in that year having but one room with a plank floor, has in a few months increased to a city of six thousand people; with its fine hotels, stores, manufactories, and all the appliances, comforts and many of the luxuries of civilization. . . . Lofty buildings are rising on the business streets; solid and substantial brick edifices of which old cities might well be proud. . . . Great trains of huge prairie freighters arrive and depart almost daily, and more than a thousand emigrant wagons arrive every week.

Another account of Denver in 1860 describes the miners and freighters: "Hardy, brown-faced, weatherbeaten sovereigns from the plains, the mountains, and the mines, with a profusion of buckskin patches, red shirts and hairy faces crowd every corner, fill up the stores and thickly surround the auction stands."[2] Increasing numbers of women promenaded the streets, in calico dresses and sunbonnets or the latest Paris fashions, while Arapaho Indians in buffalo robes and blankets bartered for trinkets, sugar, and whiskey.

In the first decade of Colorado mining, the two leading cities were the territorial capital, Denver, and the mining camp composed of Central City, Black Hawk, and Nevadaville. Each had two daily newspapers and three banks, as well as churches, schools, and other indications of civilization. Few larger communities elsewhere in the nation had such enterprising, accomplished populations. There were miners, merchants, operators, and gold hunters, some on the road to great wealth and others who had won and lost several fortunes already.

Life in pioneer mining camps was picturesque and fascinating. Mining was hard work, demanding muscle and endurance. The hope of striking it rich was ever present. The population of Colorado was constantly changing as optimistic new arrivals replaced disappointed miners who returned to the East or moved on to other territories.

Clothes did not distinguish the man, for all types—university graduates, doctors, lawyers, preachers, and farmers turned miners—wore substantial shirts, trousers, and boots appropriate to their heavy work. Long whiskers often hid a youthful face. There were no old people in pioneer Colorado. One early pioneer claims it was several years before he saw a person with gray hair.

Congress organized the territory of Colorado on February 28, 1861, at which time a census found the population to be 25,329, of whom 4,484 were females. Before this time Colorado lay within the boundaries of the territories of Utah, New Mexico, Nebraska, and Kansas.

Many streams were worked to great disadvantage, as some ground was divided between too many owners. Eventually, many such diggings were abandoned. Nevertheless, large quantities of gold were obtained from 1860 to 1863 from creeks, placers, and gulches alone, and the lode mines in Gilpin County, which were worked all year round, were also very productive.

Few men who came to Colorado knew anything of mining or milling, but this made little difference for placer or creek mining. When working at depths over sixty feet, however, most amateur mill men had difficulty removing the gold from refractory ores with high lead content. Above that point, where the ground had been eroded by the elements, removal was easier. Many claims were sold and much work suspended because of the miners' inability to extract the precious metal, but many mines that had not been worked too deep to get below the decomposed mineral continued paying.

During the spring of 1864, when inflation resulting from the Civil War caused a rise in the price of gold, there was considerable interest in mining investments and stocks from as far away as New York. Many mines, both good and bad, were bought up. It was a speculative era, during which wealth was acquired rapidly, and people were so anxious to possess a mine or stock in one that the supply fell short of the demand. Agents from the East were sent to Colorado to find and purchase mining claims.

In 1865–66 the boom collapsed and left the mining industry with a bad name. Working capital spent on ineffective process mills and vast amounts of machinery, high-salaried and incompetent staffs, higher freight charges due to an Indian war on the plains, as well as higher labor and supply costs caused the closing down of many companies and properties. Many miners left for new diggings in Montana and Idaho.

Gold was the only metal sought in the early years of Colorado mining; no one had thought to prospect for silver. Most of the state's mineral wealth was overlooked until 1870 and later, although rich silver ore was discovered on McClellan Mountain near Georgetown as early as 1864 and caused some lively prospecting in 1865.

From 1865 through 1870, lode mining was carried on in nearly all the gold-bearing districts then discovered. Many gave out; others, unprofitable for gold mining, were later found to be rich in silver. From 1867 through 1870 most of Colorado's gold came from Gilpin County, one of the few areas where mining operations were carried on extensively. Gilpin County might be called the mother of Colorado mining towns and camps, for many men who left the area developed new mining districts all over the mountains and influenced the direction of affairs wherever they settled.

Smelters began to be appreciated with the establishment and successful operation of the Boston and Colorado Smelting Works at Black Hawk in 1867–68. Stamp mills and smelting works became an important addition to the communities as they saved a very high percentage of the gold and silver content of the ore.

In the late 1860s several minor gold discoveries were made at California Gulch in Lake County, and a silver lode in Boulder County established a flourishing mining camp at Caribou. In the early 1870s the discovery of silver-bearing deposits in Park County, once famous for gold, led to the revival of Fairplay and Alma, and rich discoveries south of Canon City brought activity to the camp of Rosita. Many silver discoveries had been made in the mountains around Georgetown, and the yield of gold and silver there increased from 1870 on so that by 1874 the product from that area surpassed that of Gilpin County for the first time.

In the summer of 1870, the completion of the Denver Pacific Railway from Denver to Cheyenne effected a connection with the Union Pacific, which had passed Denver to the north. In August of the same year, the Kansas Pacific reached Denver, making two lines to the East. In addition, the construction of the Colorado Central Railway from Denver to Golden opened a gateway to the mountains. The building of this route from Golden to Black Hawk in Clear Creek Canyon was the turning point in mining prosperity because the reduced transportation costs made it profitable to work previously losing mines. Smelting works and improved mining and milling operations also contributed to the success of the area.

In 1872 and 1873, the San Juan region in southwestern Colorado began to attract attention, as did the great belts where the towns of Silverton (1874), Lake City (1874), and, later, Ouray (1876) grew up. Trails had to be blazed to these mining centers and roads built over rugged mountain passes and through precipitous canyons.

The census of 1870 showed Colorado's population to be 39,864, although as many as 100,000 people, many moving on, had probably lived in Colorado during the 1860s. From this time on, owing largely to the railways and the generous production of the mines, a steady migration from the East took place. The population is said to have doubled by 1874, four years after the advent of the railway. On August 1, 1876, Colorado was admitted to the Union.

Much mineral wealth was gained in 1876. Both the older counties and the more recently settled San Juan region were doing well. The succeeding year was even more prosperous as the mines made larger gains than ever before. More railway and ore-reducing facilities were being constructed; the Colorado Central Railway was extended as far as Georgetown. In 1878, the most prosperous year yet, the gold and silver yield showed a gain of nearly 50 percent over the best previous year. Financial improvement as well as population and production increases took place. The old reliable districts all surpassed their previous records, with Lake County now leading the way. For several years the production in this area had been slow, but the new lead carbonate mines of Leadville paid well in 1877 and surprised everyone with their output. By 1879 a mining boom of enormous proportions had begun, due mainly to the discovery, development, and extraordinary production of these silver deposits in

Leadville. Destitute prospectors became wealthy overnight, and men of moderate means became bonanza kings. Real estate vaulted skyward, lot jumping was common, crime was not an uncommon occurrence, and vice was open. Saloons and gambling dens drew large crowds. Everyone seemed impatient for wealth and used any means to gain it. Leadville was one of the busiest and most talked of cities in the nation. Her rapid rise and unprecedentedly wealthy mines brought prosperity to the whole state.

During this period of rapid growth and prosperity railways reached the Leadville, South Park, and Gunnison regions as well as Silverton in the San Juan region. Heavy investments of eastern and foreign capital were common. The Colorado mining product of 1879 increased a remarkable 80 percent over 1878. Colorado led the world in the production of precious metals.

Towns and camps like Leadville but smaller sprang up in the new mining areas. The bustling mining towns with their saloons, stores, and miners' cabins clung to mountainsides, squeezed into narrow canyons, or nestled in mountain-walled valleys. Some faded quickly while others continued for years.

A census in 1880 found the population to be 194,327, almost five times the 1870 population. Half the number, attracted largely by the Leadville boom, had arrived after statehood was achieved in 1876. By the end of 1880, Leadville had settled down and become quite well organized.

Prospecting continued in the 1880s as cities grew and wealth increased. Railroad building continued at a tremendous pace, connecting all parts of the state. Gold continued to be mined in slightly larger quantities than during previous decades, but the production and value of silver and lead far exceeded that of gold. Colorado was becoming known as the "Silver State." Before the silver crash in 1893, the yearly production of silver was outdistancing gold by $20,880,000 to $5,300,000.

The pioneer counties of Gilpin and Clear Creek continued consistent production while Leadville continued as principal mining center of the state, although its production was diminishing. The new mines that opened in the 1880s resulted in the rise of new cities and four additional mining counties. The discovery of silver at Nigger Baby Hill in 1879 led to the development of Rico and the creation of Dolores County in 1881 with Rico as county seat. Prospectors from Ouray and Lake City discovered rich lodes in the rugged mountains at the sources of the San Miguel River. Columbia, rechristened Telluride in 1883, was settled in 1878; it became the center of mining activity for the region and county seat of the newly organized San Miguel County in 1883. Red Cliff, settled in 1879, was the location of a smelter company and became the seat of Eagle County in 1883. Mineral discoveries on the Roaring Fork of the Colorado River in 1879 resulted in the founding of Aspen, seat of Pitkin County. Little progress was made here, however, until 1887, when the first railroad was completed. Aspen's production increased and soon exceeded that of Leadville, in a boom that lasted until the silver crash of 1893.

The railroad reached the new town of Durango in 1881. The presence of large coal veins and the favorable location of the town in relation to the mines of Silverton, Ouray, Rico, and Telluride led to the erection of important smelting works at

Durango. Although many other plants were operated during the 1880s, Leadville, Denver, Pueblo, and Durango became the chief smelting points. New smelting methods and devices were invented; the old arrastra and stamp mill of the pioneer years were replaced by complicated machinery and elaborate chemical processes.

Coal production became important in the Walsenburg and Trinidad regions in the 1880s. Anthracite coal beds around Crested Butte in Gunnison County were also opened in the 1880s. The population of the state increased from 194,327 in 1880 to 413,249 in 1890.

At the start of the 1890s the silver mines were producing greater amounts than ever before. A spectacular rush and mining boom occurred in the spring of 1890, when an important silver discovery, revealing a rich field, was struck in the southern part of the state. The new mining camp of Creede was opened in the narrow, winding canyon of Willow Creek. The great rush to this roaring camp, which began in 1891, continued with boom proportions for two years. The price of silver, however, began to fall due to oversupply and decreased coinage. As a result the Sherman Silver Purchase Act was repealed. By July of 1893 a depression of large proportions was under way throughout the United States. The panic of 1893 resulted in the closing of mines and the discharge of thousands of workers. Men who had been considered wealthy found their pockets empty. As a result of the silver collapse, hard times continued throughout 1894 for practically all classes in Colorado.

There was one bright spot in the state during this time: Cripple Creek, the last of the great mining districts in Colorado. In 1890–91, a promising vein was discovered at the site of the future great gold camps, southwest of Pikes Peak. Other mines were discovered; a mining district comprising those related mines was organized in the spring of 1891, and other camps, later to become towns, sprang up in the region. The gold output increased rapidly for this richest gold district in the United States, producing a hopeful outlook for the state. Cripple Creek was a bustling metropolis during these years. In 1896 fire destroyed the town, but it was rebuilt on a grander scale with handsome business blocks, hotels, banks, and all the features of a modern city. Mills and smelters were built nearby at Florence, Colorado City, and Victor.

Despite migration out of the state during the hard times of 1893–95, the population increased from 413,249 to 539,700. Mainly because of the Cripple Creek–Victor area mines, the total annual metal production for 1900 was the highest in the history of the state. In the early 1900s, however, mining activities decreased in the area owing to a steady decline in the value of precious metals, high production costs, and violent labor wars. Agricultural and manufacturing towns showed marked growth during this period as the mining communities faded.

Since the days of the rush to Cripple Creek there have been no similar movements except for a tungsten boom, on a much smaller scale, in the Boulder district during World War I and an interest in uranium during the 1940s and 1950s.

Today, a number of the mining towns of early days are completely deserted. Others, despite boarded-up houses and deserted stores, hold onto life, while only a few are active and reasonably prosperous.

2

Town Planning and Organization

Colorado mining communities exhibit three distinct phases of development:

(1) *Settlement Phase.* This beginning stage of all towns was characterized by the presence of log cabins and tents, crude street layouts, small populations, limited access, and few town amenities. As a result of the mad rush for rapid wealth, the initial structures were quickly constructed and randomly placed with little concern for location other than proximity to the rich ores. Some communities in poor mining districts or remote areas never got beyond this stage. Little or nothing remains of such settlements today apart from an occasional cabin.

(2) *Camp Phase.* This second stage occurred when settlement populations grew larger and mineral strikes became more promising. Sawmills were set up, frame buildings appeared, streets were laid out, city governments were established, and utilities and other amenities appeared. Architecture remained primitive; few or no stone or brick buildings appeared in these camps. Although stone was available, most mine and camp builders chose wood, despite the danger of fire, because of reduced time and effort in construction, availability of materials, and economic considerations. Some communities that were bypassed by transportation routes or whose mineral deposits proved less valuable than expected never got beyond this stage. Several examples of communities that never passed this camp level remain (fig. 2). Most of these mining camps are in a deteriorated condition, many are inaccessible, and they do not provide the most representative cross section of the society as a whole.

(3) *Town Phase.* This third stage of development occurred when a camp became an important location because of mining prosperity or its prominence as a supply center. Architecture became more elaborate as unpretentious wood structures were replaced and joined by more elaborate frame homes and public edifices built of stone and brick (figs. 3, 4, 5). Nearly all building types grew larger and brought with them

2. St. Elmo never graduated from the mining camp phase of development. Simple frame vernacular structures and wood sidewalks line the main street. Like many other camps, St. Elmo began to decline when operation of the mines became economically unfeasible and rail service was discontinued.

3. The commercial buildings of Central City, which reached the town phase of development, create an interesting silhouette of varying cornice heights.

4. The commercial district of Black Hawk, constructed of stone and brick, also represents the town stage of evolution.

5. The streets of Central City, another third-phase community, follow the irregular, hilly topography of the area.

an air of refinement and permanence. Camp amenities were enlarged and increased, and they were joined by a full range of the latest urban services available at the time. The citizens of a town began to think of themselves as city dwellers, in contrast to settlement or camp denizens who thought of themselves as frontiersmen.

Many camps were located at precipitous sites that were difficult to reach. When elbow room existed, the camps took advantage of it. In the case of Silverton, where several strikes were discovered in surrounding mountainous areas, the town evolved in a less rugged, flat valley site which was centrally located between discoveries (fig. 6).

6. Wide main streets, as seen in this view of Silverton, provided ease of movement for street activities.

7. Ouray, occupying a mountainous setting, uses the standard grid pattern of streets.

One or two main streets usually went down the center of town. Almost all commercial enterprises, such as hotels, stores, shops, and offices, were located along these thoroughfares. Generally, livery stables, industries, and other undesirable commercial ventures were located at the edge of town. Residential areas were located behind one side or both sides of the main street. The main street of a camp in a hilly location would traverse the slope, dividing the camp into an upper and a lower section. Schools, churches, and the more desirable residential lots were likely to appear on the upper levels of the town. The less desirable saloons, as well as gambling halls, the red-light district, and inexpensive housing, would be found on the lower levels, closer to the creek, river, or railroad tracks. In a town located on a flat site, the creek, river, or railroad side of the main street was generally thought of as the least desirable area.

Street layouts followed four similar arrangements. Whenever the terrain allowed, a standard grid pattern of streets was used, as in the case of Ouray (fig. 7). In Silver Plume, a modified grid pattern was used, since a creek through the middle of town altered the standard arrangement. St. Elmo exemplifies the third category, where the camp conforms to the winding stream. Finally, in Central City, the streets follow the irregular, hilly topography (fig. 5). The towns might follow any one of these arrangements or combinations thereof.

Nearly all streets were ungraded dirt, often lined with wooden sidewalks (fig. 8). The main streets of some of the fancier towns were paved, but rarely the side streets. In these towns, more permanent building materials were used for sidewalks. For example, Leadville had concrete sidewalks, Georgetown had some flagstone sidewalks and also street elevators, while Cripple Creek had many brick sidewalks (fig. 9). Whenever the terrain allowed, wide streets, sometimes as wide as sixty feet, were common (fig. 6). This allowed for ease in turning around of freight wagons and packtrains, and provided ample space for all street activities.

8. Wooden sidewalks offered protection from muddy streets. This example is in the early camp of St. Elmo.

9. Prosperous towns featured sidewalks of more permanent materials than the wood walks found in camps. This decorative brick example is in Cripple Creek.

Streets were crowded with activity day and night. Animal and vehicular traffic interfered with a pedestrian's freedom of movement. Cripple Creek's solution to that problem was to rope off its main street from 2 P.M. every day until the next morning for pedestrian use only. Horse-drawn—and later, in some towns, electric—streetcars, as well as horses, were used for transportation in town.

The panorama of the main street included commercial structures with unique and irregular silhouettes of varying cornice heights and treatments (figs. 3, 4, 5). Storefronts adjoined each other, and their flush fronts marched parallel down both sides of the main street. A handsome addition to the streetscape was the appearance of gas streetlighting. After gaslights came to Leadville in 1879 the town was nicknamed "Leadville by Lamplight." Electric streetlights made their first appearance in Aspen in 1888.

Except in rare cases where the first arrivals rejected them, saloons were among the first businesses organized in a camp, along with general stores which provided food staples and mining supplies. White Pine, a typical small camp of the 1880s, had a hotel, theater, city hall, store buildings and sheds, a boardinghouse for miners, and frame dwellings. Lake City in 1881 boasted two banks, three smelting works, two drugstores, three breweries, a public library, one newspaper, one newstand, five general stores, two bakeries, two blacksmith shops, two sawmills, three restaurants, one livery stable, a millinery store, one shoe shop, two meat markets, and five saloons.

Restaurants, gambling halls, and saloons were often open twenty-four hours a day. Many of the towns in their beginning stage had a wide open, devil-may-care character. About half the population of some early camps was made up of pickpockets, mining sharks, gamblers, saloon keepers, con artists, prostitutes, and other unsavory characters. Efforts to bring law and order were sometimes difficult, and shootings were not uncommon.

Advertising campaigns were often used to influence people to come to the towns. This type of campaigning was partly responsible for the flood of people into Leadville, which grew as if by magic. In May 1878, the population was fifteen hundred and by the end of the decade it was over twenty-five thousand. In 1878 Helen Hunt Jackson wrote:

> In six months a tract of dense, spruce forest had been converted into a bustling village. To be sure, the upturned roots and the freshly hacked stumps of many of the spruce trees are still in the streets . . . the houses are all log cabins, or else plain unpainted board shanties. . . . The Leadville places of business are another thing; there is one compact, straight street, running east and west, in the center of this medley of sage brush, spruce stumps, cabins and shanties. . . . The middle of the street was always filled with groups of men talking. Wagons were driven up and down as fast as if the street were clear. It looked all the time as if there had been a fire, and the people were just dispersing, or as if town meeting were just over. Everybody was talking, nearly everybody gesticulating. All faces looked restless, eager, fierce. It was a Monaco gambling room emptied into a Colorado spruce clearing.[1]

By the end of 1878, the streets of Leadville were lined with frame buildings. A year later, the Clarendon Hotel, the Opera House, and other brick buildings were standing along Harrison Avenue.

Although there was some prefabrication, the rapid growth of the towns, without benefit of formal planning, was made possible by the invention of balloon framing, where studs or uprights run from sill to eaves with horizontal members nailed to them. "A freight load of lumber delivered in the morning meant a new place of business by night," according to one historian.[2] Many people tore their houses down and took them with them when they moved. The scarcity of lumber in some places caused other buildings to be used as firewood.

Residents of the early towns were glad to greet the newcomers and to sell or rent them lots, houses, shops, or whatever else they might need. Real estate was big business. In some camps, for merchants with tents, vacant lots rented at from $25.00 to $50.00 per month. When the town of Columbia (Telluride) was platted, the town board sold lots for $3.50 to induce people to move to town and build homes, while in other camps lots were given away, along with water and firewood, to anyone who would agree to grade one-half the width of his own street along his frontage. By contrast, lots in some towns were sold for $750.00 or more. In Creede, for example, where lots were offered at outrageous prices, some settlers outsmarted the scalpers by building shacks supported on planks laid across Willow Creek.

As historian Duane Smith points out, "The mining camp represents something different and, for the most part, new in the American frontier experience: urbanization. . . . Urbanization meant that the problems which faced the settled regions were transported to the frontier and placed in an entirely new environment."[3] As the camps grew, congestion and overbuilding were common, as in the cases of Black Hawk, Central City, and Nevadaville, which were spread together up and down the gulch, laid out with no plan whatsoever. Buildings almost stood on top of each other. "It was a common complaint of the quid-chewing fraternity that no man dare to spit out his front door for fear of hitting his neighbor's chimney and putting out the fire."[4]

Urbanization brought with it the need for city utilities. As previously mentioned, some towns had gas-lighting in the streets and for houses and businesses by the late 1870s. Gas was provided by local gasworks. Electricity took over from gas in the 1880s (fig. 10). The Healy house installed electricity in 1884, one of the first buildings in Leadville to have it.

Until an adequate city water system could be set up, water wagons were used. Water sold for fifty cents per barrel in early Leadville, thirty buckets for a dollar in early Victor. Cottonwood logs, hollowed out, served as early waterlines. With city improvements came waterworks and hydrant installation. The hydrants were partic-

10. This early electric power pole in the camp of St. Elmo is attached to a commercial false front.

ularly necessary for fire fighting. Sewer systems, however, were practically nonexistent. The early sewer line for the Strater Hotel in Durango was square and wooden; it was buried under the railroad tracks and ran into the river.

In 1860, the owners of the Pikes Peak Stage Line established the Pony Express. Two years later, when the telegraph line was constructed, it was discontinued. Telegraph lines were in all towns before the advent of the telephone, but lines often went down in winter. Telephones became common in the 1880s. Leadville had both the telegraph and a telephone exchange connecting most of the large business establishments with a central switchboard.

A negative aspect of urbanization was pollution. Air pollution appeared as mining activities increased. Smelter fumes were a common killer of shrubs and trees, resulting in rock and gravel yards. Partly for this reason and also because miners didn't have time for them, few parks existed. Water pollution was a constant problem due to mining activities and sewage. Noise pollution was another annoying fact of life. An early visitor wrote about Creede, "I couldn't sleep with all the noise . . . hollering, yelling, horses galloping, wagons chuckling, hammering, pounding, sawing, shooting."[5]

Livestock was free to roam. Burros were a big problem; in the winter they were turned loose to forage and would bray all night, keeping everyone awake. Packs of dogs contributed to the chorus. Newspaper editors and city hall were deluged with irate citizens' complaints.

Much more material is available on the town planning of these mining communities. A full discussion of the subject could probably fill a book in itself. It is hoped that this short chapter will provide a better understanding of the architecture examined below. The growth of these towns is fascinating in its own right; as one modern authority says, it "reflects the frontier struggle of man to build something lasting in a strange and frequently hostile environment. It becomes a story of the men and women who lived and died there, who called it home."[6]

PART II

Architecture

"The true basis for any serious study of the art of Architecture still lies in those indigenous, more humble buildings everywhere that are to Architecture what folklore is to literature or folk song to music and with which academic architects are seldom concerned."

—Frank Lloyd Wright

3
Influencing Architectural Styles

The term *Victorian* indicates a period of time, not a style. During the Victorian era many styles and combinations of styles were popular as one revival succeeded another. New building techniques, studies in Europe, and photographic books were partially responsible for the appearance of many new styles. An architect of the 1840s or later was likely to practice in more than one of several styles of the time.

In a larger sense, Victorian architecture does have its own style:

> . . . Victorian buildings are perfect symbols of an era which was not given to understatement. They are in complete harmony with the heavy meals, strong drink, elaborate clothes, ornate furnishings, flamboyant art, melodramatic plays, loud music, flowery speech, and thundering sermons of mid-19th century America.[1]

Our discussion of the architectural styles employed in the mining communities begins with the Greek Revival. The earlier Colonial, Georgian, and Federal styles that flourished on the eastern seaboard in the eighteenth and early nineteenth centuries occurred far too early to influence the mining towns of Colorado. Some of these styles, such as the Colonial, were revived later. Nevertheless, log cabins reminiscent of the earliest structures of colonial times were popular in Colorado at first because they were easily built out of readily available lumber. We will examine log structures at greater length below. On the other hand, forms unfamiliar to the East, such as western vernacular, including the western false front, were prevalent and will be discussed separately.

Greek Revival

The Greek Revival was very popular in the East from the 1820s to the 1840s. Its symmetrical design and straight-edged, white-painted facade sharply contrasted to the surrounding landscape. Greek detailing in varying degrees of accuracy was applied to the facade. The low, triangular pediment became the trademark of the style, in the form of gables and lintels. Monumental porticos and colonnades were popular additions. Owing in part to endless repetition as well as to new aesthetic insights, the style lost its popularity in the 1840s, but it straggled along until the 1850s before it disappeared entirely in the East. Greek Revival remained popular in the South until the Civil War and in the Midwest until the 1870s.

The style disappeared in the East before the earliest attempts at mining in Colorado, but its influence was felt nevertheless as miners came west from other areas. Although no pure examples of the Greek Revival appear in these towns, a frontier adaptation of Greek detailing was present. The pedimental lintel used over doorways and windows was a simple detail that could be added to the otherwise plain log and vernacular structures.

Later Victorian houses broke free from the tight, rectangular, often symmetrical Greek Revival plan in favor of a new, free, asymmetrical plan. Planned from the inside out, the layout of rooms determined the outward appearance of the building. Interior plans took on a dynamic quality, and new external features appeared in profusion.

Gothic Revival

The introduction of Gothic Revival resulted in part from romantic interest in the crumbled ruins of the medieval castles and abbeys of England. The pictorial quality of the Neo-Gothic style and its ability to fit harmoniously into settings of mountains, hills, or woods attracted architects. From the 1830s on, Andrew Jackson Downing, an American landscape architect, popularized Gothic house designs and architect Calvert Vaux designed Gothic homes that ranged from simple cottages to mock castles of stone. The Gothic Revival was also popular for churches and schools. This romantic style, characterized by irregular mass, steep central gables, and long narrow windows, often accented by lancet windows, chimneys, and porches, flourished in the East until the time of the Civil War.

In the East, houses of this style were often constructed of stone. Only wealthy men could afford such homes, which required the labors of highly skilled stone carvers. The costly Gothic style could be translated into wood, however; in the mining towns narrow exposed lap siding and board-and-batten siding were the most frequent exterior treatments, and stone tracery became wooden "gingerbread":

Gothic, a massive style copied after the cathedrals of Europe, had lines that translated surprisingly well into wood—the cathedral high-arched windows, the sharp gables filled in with carved cross bars and fretted bargeboards, the vertical board-and-battens. Gothic had been a particularly fitting style for churches because of its upward lines, its spires and elevated arches, all pointing the way to heaven. . . .[2]

In addition to the relatively elaborate examples of this style found in the mining communities, regional adaptations appear in the form of bits of Gothic detailing on log and vernacular structures. The Gothic Revival style is found in the mining towns after the Civil War years during which it died in the East. Churches remained faithful to the Gothic Revival even later, as the style was thought to be natural for religion.

Italianate

Roughly simultaneous with the Gothic Revival was the equally strong revival of Italian Renaissance architecture. In the East, the brownstone, the suburban "Hudson River Bracketed" house, and the country "Tuscan Villa" were manifestations of this taste. Rooms were often grouped by function, producing an irregular perimeter. The style was characterized by its unsymmetrical plan, shallow-hipped roof with elaborate bracket-supported overhang, balconies, loggias, and towers. The Italianate style, in contrast to the Greek Revival, could be added to in all directions. In addition to its popularity in residential structures, the Italian style replaced the Grecian for official and commercial architecture. As early as the 1840s many commercial and official buildings were patterned after Italian palazzos. The use of cast-iron, self-supporting fronts for multistoried commercial structures became popular in the late 1840s, quickly came into use throughout the country, and lasted about twenty-five years.

In the mining towns, the masonry interpretation of the Italianate style used in the East was often translated into less costly frame and clapboard construction. Although the style's influence on residential designs was less evident in Colorado than in other parts of the country, less elaborate cube-shaped adaptations with bracketed projecting roof overhangs were occasionally found. On the other hand, the corniced and bracketed design, translated into wood, cast iron, and brick, was very popular for commercial architecture. Because of the usual time lag and because it was so adaptable to commercial structures, the Italian influence lasted longer in the mining communities than it did in the East.

French

Paris had long been thought of as the artistic capital of the western world, and as traveling architecture students returned from that city they brought with them many French practices and tastes. The hallmark of the French style was the mansard roof, named after the seventeenth-century architect François Mansart. With its four steep sides and flatter upper slopes broken by large dormer windows, the mansard roof was practical as well as decorative; it utilized wasted attic space and circumvented European height restrictions. Beginning in the late 1850s the French style dominated both public and private American architecture in the East. The roof was also adaptable to other styles and often was placed on top of Gothic Revival and Italianate designs. Its great success and popularity diminished in the mid 1870s.

Although the mansard roof appeared occasionally in residential and institutional architecture of the mining towns, its greatest popularity was in hotel architecture in the more prosperous mining communities. The French style, with its mansard roof, dormer windows, and iron cresting, remained influential in the mining towns until the late 1880s.

Queen Anne

In an attempt to establish a national style, an American version of an English import was developed in the form of the Queen Anne house of the 1870s. Its identifying characteristics, like those of the related Eastlake and Stick styles, were contrasting shapes, irregular floor plan, complex geometry, porches, overhangs, bay windows, oriels, balconies, leaded glass, stained glass, clustered brick chimneys, dormers, turrets, towers, varying roof planes, and elaborate woodwork. The use of many different materials in the same building was popular, as was the emphasis on ornamentation. In addition, Queen Anne residential and commercial structures incorporated the earlier Panel Brick detail, which utilized brick masonry in a variety of decorative patterns by means of projecting or receding the brick panels in an attempt to animate the facade.

In the East the style began to fade about 1890. In the mining towns of Colorado the Queen Anne style was very popular well into the 1890s; elaborate examples of the style in both residential and commercial architecture are widespread.

Romanesque Revival

Parallel with the Queen Anne and often referred to as Richardsonian Romanesque after Henry Hobson Richardson, the Boston architect who was influential in establishing it in this country, the Romanesque Revival style reflected in its design the specific nature of the building materials and the structural system. Inspired by the Romanesque architecture of early medieval France, the style began to appear in the 1870s after Richardson's return from France. Richardsonian buildings were monumental, fortresslike public structures with a mood of "gloomy robustness."[3] Although many small buildings of this style were constructed of wood, with shingle roofs and walls, for the most part round masonry arches and rough-textured, rock-faced masonry wall surfaces were preferred. The popularity of the style ebbed in 1893 after the World's Columbian Exposition at Chicago, when classical influence was revived.

A few mining town commercial buildings—principally banks—were influenced by Richardsonian Romanesque because of the style's fortresslike qualities. The style remained popular in the mining towns until both the Chicago Exposition and the silver crash of 1893.

Other Revivals

Even before the Chicago Exposition, such new styles as Colonial Revival, Georgian Revival, and Federal Revival had begun to emerge in the East as the result of a growing interest in classical art. As a consequence of the silver crash of 1893, however, most of the mining towns were dead by the time the styles reached the West. In those that continued to function, the earlier styles hung on until the end of the century. Colonial Revival and Georgian Revival influences began to appear by 1900 as the awareness of classical art spread to the West.

The pioneers in the early mining settlements and camps brought with them styles that were prevalent in the East at the time. The development of communities at new strikes was influenced not only by new styles coming from the East but also by transient miners who brought with them earlier styles from previous boom areas. As a result, the mining towns were architectural melting pots in which the major styles overlapped, fused, and were sometimes combined in the same building.

As in the cases of Central City in the 1860s with its Italianate buildings, Leadville in the late 1870s and early 1880s with a mixture of Italianate, French, and Queen Anne structures, and Cripple Creek in the 1890s with Queen Anne and Colonial Revival influences, mining towns at parallel stages of evolution differed from decade to decade as a result of varying technological advances and changing architectural styles.

4

Residential Architecture

The architecture of the residential structures evolved through many styles. Beginning with the log cabin, followed by the vernacular and western false front forms and the previously mentioned influences from Greek Revival to Colonial Revival, our discussion will follow generally the sequence in which these styles appeared in the towns.

Log Cabins

When miners first settled an area, they usually lived in tents before building more permanent homes. Aside from an occasional adobe dwelling, solitary log cabins or combinations of log and canvas were the first permanent structures on the mining frontier (fig. 11). Trees were plentiful, and the structures could be quickly erected without nails. An ax was the only necessary tool. Most log cabins were built like their eastern counterparts, with knowledge brought from the East. Logs were first notched at each end so they would fit together better. Then they were often flattened or hewn on the top and bottom and sometimes on all four surfaces to a rectangular cross section (figs. 12, 13, 14). The first four logs were laid flat on the ground unless a floor was desired, in which case foundation logs were placed on stones on top of which floor members could rest. Supported by the log below and reinforced by the weight of the one above, each log was held in place. If no tools were available to flush the corners, the ends of the logs usually extended beyond the corners. Spaces between the logs were filled with small pieces of wood, stones, moss, wet clay, or sometimes animal hair or straw. A log skeleton of a pitched roof was covered with tree limbs, canvas, earth, shingles, or sheet metal.

26

11

11. This primitive one-room log cabin in Matterhorn is typical of early miners' residences.

12. Square notching of logs, as seen in this Ironton example, was one of many methods used in cabin building.

13. As this cabin in Breckenridge shows, logs were sometimes intricately spliced to increase their horizontal length.

14. The spaces between the logs of this cabin in St. Elmo have been filled by the chinking method.

12

13

14

Typical early cabins were one room about fourteen feet square, with a dirt floor, one window, and a fireplace, which provided warmth, illumination, and a source of heat for cooking. Early chimneys and fireplaces were constructed of mud, limbs, and small logs; later, they were built of stone or brick. Cast-iron coal- or wood-burning stoves, however, were cheaper and easier to install than stone fireplaces and consequently were more popular when available. Many miners froze to death through failure to keep an adequate supply of wood on hand for a long cold snap.

Although glass was available, it was costly, so animal skins, sliding boards, and greased paper were often used in window openings. Front doors made of wood slabs opened outward to allow more room on the inside and were sometimes swung on wood hinges or strips of animal skin. Water was usually drawn from a nearby stream, and the supply was sometimes supplemented by a cistern fed by rainspouts. Illumination was by fire and candle. The toilet facilities were the outdoors until the appearance of the outhouse.

One of the first cabins in Denver was described as follows in 1858:

> We have a nice door with an old-fashioned wooden latch, with the string on the outside of course. The fireplace, as is the custom in this country, is made of sods. In the southeast corner is the bunk; in the northwest corner the window, four panes of glass with sash. On the north side, between the end of the bed and the fireplace, we have two shelves and a bench, all made with a nice slab. We cut the meat on the bench and set water buckets on the other two shelves. . . . On the northeast side and corner we hang our coats, guns, and things. . . . You have no idea how comfortable we all live. We sleep warm and nice.[1]

The simple furnishings of the log cabins were handmade by the residents. A. D. Richardson, a pioneer journalist, wrote: "Chairs were glories yet to come. Stools, tables and pole bedsteads were the staple furniture, while rough boxes did duty as bureaus and cupboards."[2] Pine boughs were often used for mattresses and buffalo robes for covers.

During mining days cabins were always kept stocked with food and fuel. In case of bad weather, anyone needing shelter was free to use the nearest cabin, as people were generally friendly to the traveler.

The two-room cabin with a front living area and rear kitchen was a popular phase of the log cabin development. Many such cabins had lofts, which were later developed into a second story (figs. 15–18). Log additions or shed projections were often built onto the rear and used as kitchens, thus providing additional interior space (fig. 19).

Exterior detailing was almost nonexistent, but occasionally a board topped by a low triangular profile to recall a Greek pediment was placed over a door or window (fig. 20). As sawmills appeared when a settlement prospered, the log cabins were either replaced by frame structures of balloon construction, covered with lap siding, or expanded with frame additions, which resulted in the early vernacular forms of residential mining town architecture (figs. 21, 22).

15. Log residences were added to vertically as well as horizontally to provide additional interior space. This one-and-one-half-story cabin is in Breckenridge.

16. Shed projections to the rear of many cabins also provided more interior space. In many one-and-one-half-story houses, the loft was expanded to provide additional bedroom area in the two-story version. This example is in Lake City.

Vernacular

The term *vernacular architecture* does not have a stylistic connotation but refers simply to things that are native or homemade. Vernacular or indigenous buildings are those constructed according to local traditions and climatic conditions. Although log cabins could be included in this category, they have been discussed separately for the sake of clarity.

When sawmills began converting the timber into rough, green planks, board buildings replaced the earlier log structures. Board shacks, both single and double layered, were followed by more substantial frame houses. These resembled the one-

17. This log has been notched to receive second-story floor joists. Fig. 18 shows the usage of such a log.

18. Floor joists, supporting the second story, protrude through this cabin wall in St. Elmo.

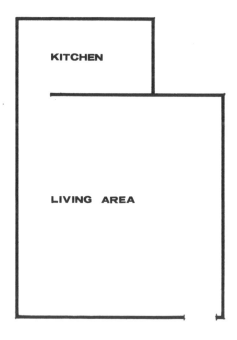

19. The kitchens of early log and frame dwellings were often removed from the original plan and added to the rear as a projection to provide more interior living space.

20

21

22

20. A simple Greek pedimental lintel tops the window of this log cabin in St. Elmo. Detailing of this nature on log structures was rare.

21. This log building in Breckenridge was partially covered with lap siding after sawmills began to operate in the area.

22. With the appearance of sawmills, frame projections were often added to log structures like this St. Elmo cabin.

and two-room log structures, the most familiar form to use as a guide (fig. 23). As was done in the log cabins, the living and kitchen spaces of the one-story frame were expanded by loft and attic space in the one-and-one-half-story, which in turn were used for additional sleeping areas in the two-story (fig. 24). In addition, as in the case of the log cabin, a shed projection was often added to the rear to provide additional interior space.

While the basic form remained the same, the entrances of many frame structures were built on the pitch side of the roof rather than the gable end (fig. 25). With the

23. Early frame houses like this example in Ironton followed the plan of earlier log cabins.

24. Early frame dwellings were expanded in the same ways as log cabins, as seen in this one-and-one-half-story vernacular home in Crested Butte.

familiar shed projection to the rear, the resulting form was not unlike a modified eastern colonial saltbox (fig. 26).

Stone foundations remained, and the heavy-timbered braced frame construction used earlier in the East was replaced by balloon framing, in which thin upright studs were nailed to horizontal joists and diagonal braces. This form of construction allowed for rapid building. In addition to plank siding over the skeletal frame, clapboards or horizontal overlapping wooden boards, and vertical board-and-batten siding were used. Board-and-batten, shingle, or metal covering over the pitched, and

25. This simple frame vernacular house of the side-entrance type is in Alma.

26. Another plain vernacular example in Alma with similar side entrance recalls the shape of the colonial saltbox with its projection to the rear.

occasional hip, roof was common. Although nails were available, window frames were often put together with wooden pegs. Sawdust was commonly used for insulation; newspaper, canvas, and cloth, as well as wallpaper, were popular for wall and ceiling coverings.

Water was sold by the bucket and barrel as well as being collected from streams and cisterns. Fireplace and candle illumination were supplemented by the introduction of coal oil and kerosine lamps. Simple shack outhouses of vertical plank construction were built close to the main house. These small square or rectangular

27. A primitive outhouse in the camp of St. Elmo.

structures with shed or pitched roofs, often a window in the door, and one or two seats provided adequate toilet facilities (fig. 27).

As in the case of log cabins, exterior ornamental detail was basically nonexistent, but as elements of the styles prevalent in the East reached the mining communities, the vernacular forms adopted some of their details. These transitional vernacular forms are actually territorial and frontier adaptations of the eastern styles and will be discussed accordingly with their respective styles.

The western false front, which gained great popularity for commercial buildings of the period, was rarely applied to residential architecture. In the few homes where they appeared, the fronts were added to or combined with the vernacular form (figs. 28, 29). Because of its limited contribution to residential structures, further discussion of the false-front style has been reserved for the section on commercial architecture.

Victorian Era Styles

The Victorian era saw many styles and combinations of styles as one revival succeeded another. The period brought with it, to the mining towns as well as the East, irregular, more complex floor-plan and elevation arrangements, in contrast to the

28. A false-fronted residence in the South Park City Museum (Fairplay) with a simple bracketed cornice and Greek pediments over the windows.

29. This elaborate false-fronted house in Leadville displays a decorative bracketed cornice and fanciful porch.

earlier simple, symmetrical vernacular forms. The exterior often displayed exuberant color and elaborate decoration.

The Victorian floor plan was characterized by high-ceilinged spaces and a hide-and-seek atmosphere. Toward the front entrance, in addition to the entrance hall, there was often a sitting room, where the family gathered, and the parlor, a cold, formal place, seldom used except for funerals, weddings, or when guests arrived. Very close friends were usually entertained in the sitting room and others in the parlor. The kitchens were almost always at the back of the house, usually behind the dining room. Some very large houses had two kitchens, one for the winter inside the house and one in the back for the summer, so that the interior of the house would not be overheated.

In a few houses, the kitchen was in the basement, under the first-floor dining room, and the food was brought up in a dumbwaiter. This plan was very popular in New York and Boston townhouses. The more complex plans usually corresponded to the later town phase of development.

The staircases of the houses from the 1860s through the early 1880s, leading to the upper floor bedrooms, tended to be straight and unadorned, rising from narrow entrance hallways running almost the length of the house (see below, figs. 42, 52, 59). In more elaborate Victorian houses the stairs are more ornate and wider, and, in accord with Queen Anne concepts, they sometimes ascend to the upper floors in one or two landings. Entrance halls became larger, rectangular or square (see below, fig. 62). Tall ceilings were common, for they gave more light and a feeling of grandeur. Ceilings sometimes varied in height from floor to floor; usually the first-floor ceiling was the highest. As usual, the homes of the East set the style and the West followed suit.

Interior design featured hardwood floors covered with throw rugs and in some cases, following the pre–Civil War trend in the East, wall-to-wall carpeting. Decorative patterned wallpaper was often used throughout the house, except in the kitchen, where oilcloth was favored. Prefabricated plaster ornaments such as cornices and medallions were glued in place, and decorative moldings and millwork of fine woods were also popular additions to the Victorian home.

Standard Victorian parlor furnishings included secretaries for holding books, desks, library tables, fainting couches, parlor sets, pianos, paintings by the lady of the house, and grandfather clocks (figs. 30, 31). The dining room included the dining room table, sideboards, fine china, crystal chandeliers, and diamond dust mirrors (figs. 32, 33). Bedrooms had iron, brass, or fine wood bedroom suites, high bedsteads, hand-carved wardrobes (built-in closets were nonexistent until late in the century), marble-topped dressers, washstands, small tables, rocking chairs, velvet furnishings, handmade quilts, and birdcages. Kitchen furnishings included coal ranges, pot-and-pan racks, soapstone sinks, cupboards or pantries, bread boxes, and handicrafts.

The mechanization of brickmaking, stonecutting, and woodworking allowed for many advances in construction. Balloon framing remained the most popular method of residential construction. Bricks were used, but not as commonly as in the East. They were expensive and their use called for additional time and effort in construction; furthermore, lumber was available and the popular styles of architecture were easily adapted to wood. Brick was more widely used in commercial than residential structures. Sawdust was still effective and popular as insulation, and lath and plaster walls were common.

The greatest contribution of the Victorian age to residential architecture was to supply ample light, heat, and water to the home. Victorian houses were the first to feature central heating by warm-air furnaces, hot and cold running water, cooking ranges, and indoor toilets, all of which were in use by the 1870s. Early heat sources, coal stoves or fireplaces in every room, were eventually replaced in fancy homes by coal furnaces, as home heating moved from the living quarters to the cellar. As in the

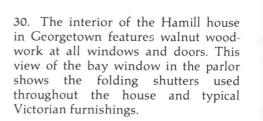

30. The interior of the Hamill house in Georgetown features walnut woodwork at all windows and doors. This view of the bay window in the parlor shows the folding shutters used throughout the house and typical Victorian furnishings.

31. The Victorian furnished dining room of the Healy house, Leadville, adjoins the smoking room, seen here to the rear.

Tabor house in Leadville, openings were often cut in the first-floor ceiling for warm air to pass to the second story. Although gas was already used for cooking and heating in the East, in the mining communities coal- and wood-burning stoves remained most common for cooking. In the 1870s, however, gas-illuminated chandeliers and wall lamps appeared in many of the finer houses. Cisterns and wells continued to supply water until, in the larger, more prosperous towns, waterworks brought in piped water. Outhouses in the style of the main house—some quite elaborate—were replaced in the more prosperous areas with indoor bathrooms. The water closet was a later addition

32. Light and dark wood strips alternate in the striped floor of the dining room of the Hamill house, Georgetown. Popular throughout the country, such hardwood floors were usually walnut, cherry, or oak, sometimes combined with pine.

33. The fireplace in Mrs. Healy's room, with typical Victorian furnishings, on the second floor of the Healy house in Leadville.

to the simple wood and box bathtubs and showers, which were already a feature of many Victorian homes. Wood-encased zinc tubs appeared in the finer residences. In many houses, the bathroom was a frame projection from the main building and often could not be used in winter because the pipes froze and burst. Cesspools were commonly used, as city sewer systems were rare.

The Victorian era, during which most of the mining towns existed, had a tremendous effect on their architecture. Styles that had taken many years to evolve in the East all appeared within a relatively short period of time in the mining communities, creating a unique architectural mixture.

GREEK REVIVAL

Greek Revival was the first of the styles prevalent in the East to appear in the mining communities. Although the style had long since gone out of fashion in the East, its influence reached the mining towns through time lag and the nostalgic memories of the eastern miners. No pure examples of the style appeared, but frontier echoes of the Greek influence occurred in the form of such ornamental trim as pedimental lintels and architraves over door and window openings, pilaster boards at corners, and overdoor lights and sidelights applied to otherwise plain vernacular buildings (figs. 34–39).

GOTHIC REVIVAL

As in the case of the Greek Revival, the first applications of the Gothic Revival in the mining communities were territorial adaptations of the characteristic Gothic details to the vernacular forms (fig. 40). Purer examples of the revival appeared as the earlier stone models were translated into less expensive wood, resulting in the emergence of the so-called Carpenter Gothic style (fig. 41). Floor plans grew more complicated as additional interior spaces were introduced (fig. 42). The addition of exterior balconies and porches also contributed to the growing irregularity of the plans. Tall, steep-pitched gable roofs appeared, with an occasional cross gable to add to the complexity. The familiar pointed arch windows, ground-floor bay windows, and upper-floor oriel windows made their appearance (figs. 43, 44). In addition to forming a pleasant sun trap during the winter months and providing a better view down the long streets, the projecting windows emphasized the plastic quality of the house

34. Greek pediments have been added to the window detailing of this simple frame vernacular house in Silver Plume. The stone foundation is clearly visible.

35. Greek detailing in the form of pediments over the windows, overdoor lights, and sidelights around the central doorway have been added to this otherwise simple vernacular house in Central City.

36

38

39

36. Greek pediments are located over the windows and overdoor lights of this vernacular house in Breckenridge.

37. This home in Silver Plume displays elaborate Greek window detailing.

38. An overdoor light and Greek pediment enhance this door in Georgetown.

39. Simple Greek window detailing adorns this house in Ironton.

37

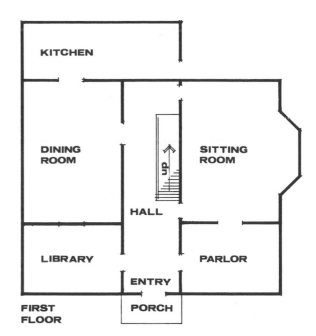

40. This simple vernacular house in Georgetown features Gothic detailing. Tudor dripstones of wood are located over the first-floor openings and over the second-floor lancet windows.

41. This Carpenter Gothic house in Lake City displays decorative window and door detailing, a pierced apron, and a finial at the roof apex.

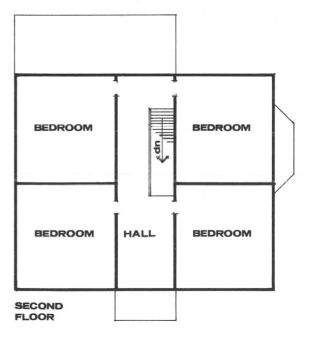

42. A typical early Victorian floor plan includes a central hallway with staircase flanked by living spaces on both floors, the kitchen lying to the rear of the first floor.

43. Second-story balustrade and pointed-arch tracery window with dripstone cap, Hamill house, Georgetown.

44. This Gothic-detailed house in Black Hawk features a ground-floor bay window, a second-story triple lancet window with leaded glass, and a bracketed roof overhang.

design. The embellishments of the exterior elevations were characteristic of the Gothic tradition. Dripstones of wood over the windows recalled the Tudor detailing of sixteenth-century England; decorative bargeboards covered the ends of the gable rafters, re-creating the fanciful stone tracery of the Gothic style into wooden "gingerbread"; ornamental triangular panels or pierced aprons at the gable apex and decorative spires or finials at the peak of the roof also added to the storybook quality of the houses. Shingles with scalloped, pointed, or dog's-tooth edges, mass-produced by local sawmills, were often placed in decorative patterns in a gable space, further enlivening the exterior surface (figs. 40, 45, 46). Decorative bracketed hoods appeared over entrances, and exterior shutters, which conflicted with the increasing window ornamentation, went out of use. Both horizontal clapboard and vertical board-and-batten siding were popular exterior wall treatments.

The Gothic Revival in the mining towns is exemplified both by elaborately detailed and by less decorative, more severe examples (figs. 47, 48). Although an occasional brick example of the Gothic can be found, wood was the most successful and popular translator of the style.

The purest and most elaborately detailed remaining example of the Carpenter Gothic is found in Black Hawk. The Lace House, built in the 1860s by the Osburn family, is replete with gingerbread, including elaborately hand-carved bargeboards and porch (fig. 49). The two-story, board-and-batten-sided structure sits, like many others, on a stone foundation. The first floor has a living room, dining room, kitchen, pantry, storage room, and one bedroom; three bedrooms are located on the second floor. Coal stoves provided heat.

45

46

47

45. An elaborate pierced apron on a house in Rico.

46. An animated gable with pierced apron and scalloped shingles, Telluride.

47. A Gothic house in Georgetown with characteristic steep-pitched roof line, finials at the apex, and bay window.

Although many fine ones exist, a good example of the less decorative Gothic Revival treatment can be found in the expensive Hamill house in Georgetown (fig. 50). Built in 1867 and added to in 1879, the two-and-one-half-story frame home of William A. Hamill, a wealthy silver speculator, rests on a stone foundation. The steep-pointed gable roof with central cross gable, the arched tracery window, and the simple detailing of the porch and balcony blend with the matching bay and oriel windows, the intermittent dormers, and the solarium of the later addition. Heated through registers by a basement furnace, the first floor has a parlor, library, solarium, dining

48. This many-gabled Gothic house in Fairplay has a two-story hexagonal bay window.

49. The Lace House in Black Hawk, built in the 1860s, is one of the purest examples of Carpenter Gothic in Colorado. Its fine wood details include board-and-batten siding, fanciful bargeboards, and elaborate wood lace on the porch.

50. The Hamill house in Georgetown, built in 1867, is a more severe, less decorative Gothic building than the Lace House. The hexagonal bay window matches the oriel window of the 1879 addition. Note also the scattered dormer windows, dripstones over the windows, and decorative rear porch and side canopy. The glassed-over solarium is part of the 1879 addition.

room, kitchen, and servants' quarters (figs. 30, 32, 51). The second floor has the master bedroom, two smaller bedrooms, a nursery, and an indoor bathroom with a marble sink and zinc bathtub; the third floor has a schoolroom and storage space (figs. 52, 53). An Italian tile fireplace in the parlor and additional fireplaces on the second and third floors supplemented the heat from the furnace. Gold-plated doorknobs and walnut doors and frames add to the aristocratic atmosphere. A granite office building and stable are at the rear of the property, as well as a spectacular six-seater outhouse in the same Gothic style as the main house.

The Hamill outhouse exemplifies the extent to which the outdoor toilet facility had evolved before its inclusion in the main-house floor plan. Beginning as small shacks, the one- and two-hole outhouses developed in the styles of the houses they served, culminating in the elaborate treatment illustrated by the Hamill outhouse, with its ventilating cupola and its bracketed, cantilevered overhang above the door (figs. 54, 55). Two-story outhouses have been claimed by Crested Butte and Silver Lake, near Silverton; the upper level was used in heavy snow during the winter. Creede had outhouses hanging over the creek, so the waste could drop directly into the water.

51. The solarium on the first floor of the Hamill house, Georgetown, was added to the original building in 1879.

52. Following the popular early Victorian floor plan, the main staircase of the Hamill house, Georgetown, ascends to the second floor from a central hallway. Light penetrates the space through a pointed-arch tracery window.

53. The comfortable interior bathroom of the Hamill house, Georgetown, includes a marble sink and a zinc-lined bathtub.

54. A primitive outhouse in the camp of Ironton.

55. This elaborate six-seater Gothic out-house behind the Hamill house in George-town features a ventilating cupola at the top and a bracketed hood over the entrance.

The Gothic Revival greatly influenced the architecture of the mining communities. The effects were widespread as churches and schools as well as homes were affected by the Gothic style. Many fine Gothic dwellings can still be found throughout the mining towns.

ITALIANATE

The Italian influence in residential architecture, although great in other parts of the country, had little effect in the mining towns. The characteristic "Italian Villa," with its flat-topped tower at the corner of an L-shaped plan, was popular for large residences in the East but was probably too complicated and expensive for Colorado and was rarely seen in the mining communities (fig. 56). More common, however, was a simpler, boxlike version, characterized by a four-sided hip roof with wide overhang, supported by decorative brackets and sometimes topped by a balustraded lookout or widow's walk (fig. 57). Several examples of this manifestation of the Italian influence remain in Georgetown, where they were constructed in the seventies and eighties of both wood and brick. In Central City, where Cornish miners, excellent dry stonemasons, erected several structures and walls of stone, a granite Italianate example remains (fig. 58).

Exterior detailing, other than the decorative brackets, remained simple; occasionally an Italian segmental head was placed over the windows. Floor plans, by nature square, were less irregular than those of the Gothic Revival but maintained the same general spatial relationships. The Healy house in Leadville illustrates this

56. An Italianate home in Georgetown. The **L**-shaped Italianate floor plan, with corner tower and bracketed roof overhang, is rare in mining towns. This is not a pure example of the Italian style, for Greek window and door detailing has also been used.

57. This more typical example of Italianate architecture, located in Georgetown, features segmental arch lintels over the windows, bracketed roof overhang, and a rooftop widow's walk.

58. This boxlike Italianate building in Central City, with bracketed roof overhang, was constructed of granite by Cornish stonemasons.

arrangement. Erected in 1878 by August R. Meyer, builder of Leadville's first reduction works, the Healy house has on the first floor a central hallway, with stairway to the second floor, flanked by a smoking room, a dining room, and a parlor, with the kitchen to the rear behind the dining room (figs. 31, 59). The second floor has two sitting room–bedroom combinations and a drawing room, on either side of the central hallway (fig. 33). Indoor bathrooms did not exist. Electricity was added to the house in 1884, as was a third floor in 1898, when the dwelling became a boardinghouse.

The Italianate style, or Bracketed style, as it is sometimes called, influenced commercial architecture more than it did residential and will be discussed in greater detail below.

48

59. Built in 1878, the Italian-influenced Healy house in Leadville follows the typical early Victorian floor plan of central hallway and staircase.

FRENCH

Such French features as the mansard roof, mansard-capped tower, and dormer windows were added to already existing floor plans, resulting primarily in an altered exterior appearance. Often combined with Italian or even Gothic detailing, the French influence was largely a matter of application of the mansard roof.

The so-called Morning Glory Mansard, a house in Leadville, was designed by architect George E. King, who was influenced enough by the French style to add a mansard roof to both the Tabor Grande Hotel and the Leadville courthouse (fig. 60). The space layout of the Morning Glory Mansard differs slightly from previously discussed floor plans in that the entrance is through the mansard-capped tower into a long and narrow foyer with stairway on the right. The plan includes the familiar living room and dining room to the left, with the kitchen to the rear. The second floor has three bedrooms, no bathrooms, a closet under the cupola, and a storage space in the cupola. A characteristic bull's-eye window adorns the tower's mansard cap.

The Maxwell house in Georgetown exemplifies the mansard roof's combination with other styles. Built by a grocer named Potter, the original simple one-story house was expanded when Potter received unexpected riches from a couple of lucky miners he had grubstaked. It is suspected that he chose the elaborate design from a Franco-Italian example in a magazine of the time. A decorative, colorful combination of French, Italian, and Queen Anne influences resulted (fig. 61). The house was later purchased by Frank Maxwell, a mining engineer. Its layout, similar to that of the Morning Glory Mansard, includes the entrance through the tower into a long hall with staircase, and a parlor, study, dining room, kitchen, breakfast room, and bath in

60. The mansard roof and tower with bull's-eye window of the Morning Glory Mansard in Leadville exemplify the French influence in residential architecture.

sequence from front to back on the left side. The second floor has five bedrooms, a sitting room, and a storage area in the cupola.

Several examples of French-influenced residential architecture still exist in a few of the mining communities. Although the mansard roof was not widely used in domestic buildings, it was popular in hotel architecture because it suggested French grandeur.

QUEEN ANNE

The return to the Queen Anne style in England was initiated by architect Richard Norman Shaw in an attempt to design houses suited to the needs of English life. This late Victorian style was greatly modified when it reached American shores. Like the similar Stick and Eastlake styles, the Queen Anne emphasized ornamentation so heavily that almost every square foot of the facade was occupied by some form of carving, design, or other embellishment. Many exterior materials—stone, multicolored brick, clapboard, shingles, and half timbers—were used, often varying from floor to floor. Gothic, Italian, and classical detailing were combined with new forms of ornamentation to aid in animating the exterior surfaces.

Bainbridge Bunting describes the charm of the Queen Anne style:

The plan of the Queen Anne house is informal and unsymmetrical; coziness is prized, and rooms are replete with alcoves, inglenooks, and bay windows. The house grows from the inside out; the exterior expresses the informal plan and delights in asymmetry, in a variety of steep-gabled wings which

50

61. The elaborate details of the Maxwell house in Georgetown blend the French influence with Queen Anne and Italian detailing. This building has been cited as one of the ten most outstanding Victorian houses in the United States.

protrude from the building, in large windows, and in numerous tall chimney stacks that bespeak hospitality and comfort within. Double hung windows are used because they are thought to be more convenient than casements. The element of good craftsmanship is stressed on the interior by elaborate plaster work, by paneled wainscots and overmantels, and in an abundance of turned woodwork.[3]

Figure 62 shows a typical Queen Anne floor plan.

Sometimes reminiscent of the Gothic Revival but sometimes more classical, Queen Anne detailing took the form of decorative porches with elaborately turned spindles, elaborate balconies, fanciful bargeboards, pierced aprons, and scalloped and pointed shingles for varying textural patterns. Picturesque dormer windows, diamond-shaped windows, lantern windows, stained glass, and leaded glass were popular. Sunburst reliefs, terra-cotta ornamentation, turrets, towers, iron cresting, and fanciful brackets combined with other features to create a complex, geometric silhouette (figs. 63–72).

Since numerous combinations of this wide range of detailing and ornamentation were possible, no single textbook example exists, but the variable Queen Anne form is always identifiable, as it differs greatly from any other style. One example is the Charles N. Miller home in Cripple Creek (fig. 68), built in 1896 by a lawyer who made

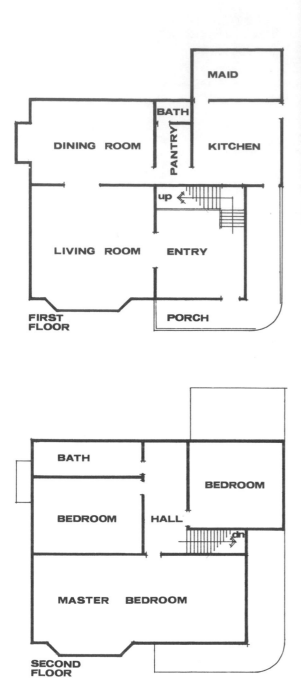

FIRST
FLOOR

SECOND
FLOOR

62

63

62. Late Victorian floor plans were more complex than their early Victorian predecessors. This typical example illustrates the informal, asymmetrical relationships between spaces.

63. This late Gothic house in Georgetown shows the complex massing that is a typical Queen Anne feature.

64. This brick house in Idaho Springs displays such characteristic Queen Anne features as complex roof plane intersections, elaborate porch detailing, and decorative chimneys.

64

65. The careful painting of this house in Ouray heightens the beautiful Queen Anne detailing.

66. This Queen Anne example in Leadville displays characteristic porches, chimneys, corner tower, and animated surfaces.

67. Another Queen Anne house in Leadville features a lantern window at the top, iron cresting along the roof line, and leaded glass windows. The original turned columns of the porch have been replaced.

68

68. The Miller house, Cripple Creek, built in 1896, shows the use of varying roof planes to add to the complexity of the Queen Anne house. The spindle porch was one of the most common features of these homes.

69. Queen Anne detailing in a gable space in Silverton. Leaded glass was common in such windows.

70. Sunburst detailing was a popular Queen Anne feature. In this beautiful example in Leadville, leaded glass has been used in the upper part of the window.

70

69

his money in mining. The first floor has a large entry hall, a large parlor with a bay window and marble fireplace, a sitting room, dining room, kitchen, pantry, maid's room, closets, and a bathroom. A handsome oak staircase leads to the second floor, where there are four bedrooms and a sitting room. The house was centrally heated and gas lighted.

Bunting describes the characteristic moldings of Queen Anne residences:

The delicate moldings and reliefs were made of an inexpensive mastic known as London Putty which would be cast in intricate designs and glued to flat wood surfaces. When covered with several coats of paint, this molded decoration could scarcely be differentiated from more expensive hand-carved trim which had also been painted.[4]

71. Towers were also common Queen Anne elements. This decorative example is on a home in Lake City.

72. This fanciful shingled tower is part of a Queen Anne house in Leadville.

Cut brick facades, in which brick masonry is used in a variety of decorative patterns, were popular in residential architecture in the East but were rarely found in the mining communities' domestic buildings. However, this adaptation of the Queen Anne style (absorbed from the Panel Brick style) was often applied to commercial structures and will be discussed as it applied to that architecture in a later section.

Queen Anne houses can still be found in the larger, more prosperous mining towns, for those who could afford such fine homes often moved to larger places. The upper classes in the smaller towns, the mining engineers, rich miners, and rich merchants, left for larger towns due to the inconveniences and hard winters of the smaller communities. A rich miner in Silverton might move to Durango, and a wealthy merchant in Central City could go to Denver, where they would own larger, fancier homes.

OTHER REVIVALS

The influence of Romanesque Revival or Richardsonian Romanesque on the residential architecture of the mining towns was very slight. It was noticeable, however, in the commercial architecture of the towns, featuring heavy, stone-faced, rusticated exteriors and rounded masonry arches.

The Colonial Revival came late to the mining communities and, like the Romanesque Revival, had little influence on the residential architecture. Its effect on commercial and institutional buildings was equally slight. No pure examples of the style resulted; rather, a colonialization of Victorian forms emerged as colonial detailing was added to earlier styles.

5
Commercial Architecture

A wide variety of business establishments flourished in the mining towns, as indicated by the *Silver Cliff Miner* in 1880: "In the way of stores and business houses, saloons of course lead, there being 25, groceries follow with 20, blacksmith 10, drygoods 8, clothing 7, meat markets 6, bakeries 6, barbershops 5, hairdressers 4, harness 4 and some 30 other places."[1] The large open spaces typical of commercial architecture could accommodate any business; the merchant's furnishings transformed the interior to his needs.

In addition to saloons, which will be discussed in another section, general stores made early appearances in the settlements. Providing food staples and mining supplies, they were a necessary addition to the communities. Before coinage, gold dust was the universal medium of exchange, usually carried on the body in some type of buckskin pouch or bag. Nearly every store or saloon had a pair of scales for weighing the gold, which was worth around eighteen dollars an ounce as it came from the sluices. If there were no scales, a pinch of dust between the thumb and forefinger was counted as twenty-five cents.

Newspapers, the primary source of communication, were also early arrivals in most towns, with type usually brought in by wagon or other conveyance. Sometimes the establishment of newspapers was difficult, as the following account indicates:

The citizens of Irwin . . . are self-reliant, honest and industrious. As an instance of what can be done, when prospects of wealth are bright, is the case of the Elk Mountain Pilot, the pioneer newspaper of the Elk Mountain country. The proprietor purchased his press, type, galleys, cases and ink, hired his type-setters, and reached the snowline on Cottonwood Pass, to the east of the mountains, to find the roads impassable, the snow deep, and not even a trail visible. The land of promise was beyond this snow-barrier . . . with hungry multitudes waiting for the newspaper, the mighty lever that moves the world.

A meeting was called by the snowbound, and a committee of the whole resolved to cross the "range," and immediately set about making snow-shoes. When each was provided with shoes, the printing material was distributed among the persons, when with type in pockets, parts of hand-press under each arm, "cases" and paper strapped on their backs, the journey across the great mountain range commenced. The ascent was made, many times at an angle of forty-five degrees, and the descent commenced, the typos gliding, gracefully down on their snowshoes, over an unknown depth of snow, in a style peculiarly western, evincing pluck, energy and perseverance, American in the extreme. The material reached Irwin safely and the first number of the Pilot was issued June 17, 1880.[2]

Most towns had at least one or two papers. Leadville had many, including an eight-page daily within two years after founding. In 1880, when the state's population was less than 200,000, there were fourteen dailies and forty-four weekly newspapers in Colorado. In the 1890s, Cripple Creek had eight newspapers, five published daily, when the city's population was about 25,000.

Because most newspapers were locally owned and edited, they were highly individualistic and colorful, much more so than modern publications. In addition to all the news, most carried racy gossip, as indicated in this reference to the daily *Creede Chronicle:* "Not everything printed could be reprinted in an eastern or family newspaper; the chronicle was not a family but a mine camp paper, but the matter that verged on the obscene attracted attention to the camp more than any other matter."[3] Mining towns were usually rough. One of the Leadville papers carried the heading "Breakfast Bullets" on almost every issue.

Many newspapers functioned as printing offices for the town, producing advertising handbills for theaters and other establishments. When newsprint was not available, newspapers were printed on practically anything; wrapping paper and even wallpaper were used.

Banks emerged as prominent commercial establishments (fig. 73). Gold and silver coins were the only currency; paper money did not exist. Robberies caused people to be afraid of keeping their money in uninsured banks. The San Miguel Bank in Telluride was once held up by the Butch Cassidy gang for $30,000, which was never recovered. By 1880 there were five banks in Leadville, two of which had deposits in excess of $2 million. Much banking business was done by mail, and there were many demands for loans. A remarkable story relates the misfortune of one bank customer:

Most San Juan banks charged for their services. One day Emil B. Fischer came into the Silverton Bank to buy a small draft. A teller made it out, said there would be no charge, and handed it to Fischer. The customer was so nonplussed by this generosity that he actually dropped dead on the spot.[4]

73. The Bank of Alma, built in 1880, is now located in the South Park City Museum (Fairplay). The plain interior includes a safe behind the tellers' cages.

Other popular businesses were stock exchanges, which dealt with the sale and purchase of mining stock, drugstores lined with shelves of medicines, and hardware stores, with shelves and boxes of building supplies (figs. 74–77). Barbershops, with rows of personal shaving mugs, offered shaves, haircuts, and baths. Post offices were besieged with long lines. Photographic studios offered pictures printed on leather to send back home. Bottled water businesses, icehouses, laundries, bakeries, hat shops, shoe shops, tailor shops, dyeing and cleaning shops, carpenter shops, liquor stores, watchmakers' shops, and jewelers' shops were common. Milk wagons ran all over the towns and even out to the mines and miners' boardinghouses. Doctors, dentists, lawyers, real estate agents, and stage line representatives maintained offices in the commercial districts, too. Other commercial enterprises, not mentioned here, will be discussed as they pertain to other categories.

74. The interior of the South Park City Museum drugstore is lined with display cases and shelves of medicines. The structure was built in Westcliffe in the 1800s.

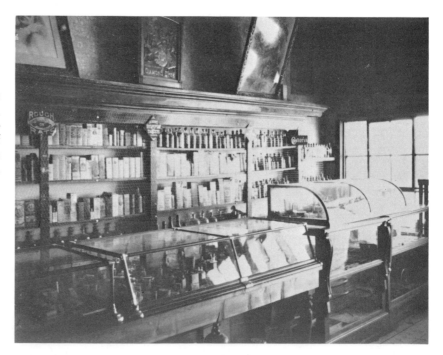

75. The Central City Pharmacy, oldest drugstore in Colorado, was built in 1874. The large glass area of the display windows and doors allows natural light to penetrate the deep commercial space.

76. The interior of an old hardware store in Leadville. The walls of the long, narrow open space are lined with boxes and drawers of building supplies.

Shops, Stores, and Offices

Like residential structures, shops, stores, and offices in the mining communities evolved through several overlapping architectural styles. Similarly, our discussion of these commercial buildings will follow the sequence in which the styles appeared in the towns.

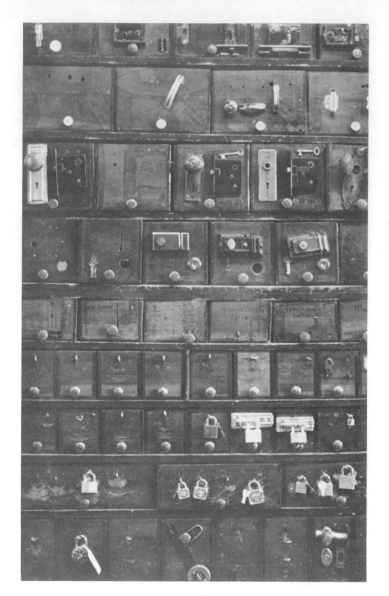

77. Storage compartments in the Leadville hardware store.

Log Buildings

In the early days, a merchant's supplies were often shipped ahead and stored in tents and canvas shelters until a building could be constructed. The merchant did business as usual out of these makeshift stores. Describing Denver in June 1860, a pioneer editor wrote:

Some are in tents, others sell from the rear end of a wagon, and others again, from a box on the sidewalk. Sacks of flour, sides of bacon, barrels of whiskey, bars of steel, fuse, blasting powder, sweet cider, fluid lightning, mining tools and an endless variety of all kinds of traps can be bought in the open air. . . . Bootmakers work in tents and the blacksmith sets up his forge in the open air. . . . Vast trains of huge wagons file through the streets and discharge their cargoes of merchandise, or pass on to the mountains with ponderous machinery that soon will drive away forever the solitude that so long has reigned.[5]

Merchants threw up log buildings, in the same form as the residential log cabins, to replace the tent structures. Boards resting on kegs served as a counter. Few remains of the early log buildings exist, as their form rapidly developed through the vernacular to the western false-front stage, or the community completely wasted away.

VERNACULAR

Like their residential counterparts, these log structures were soon boarded over with siding or gave way to neat frame structures with board floors, glass windows, and shingle roofs. Many of these small, pitched-roof buildings were comparable in their nondescript, vernacular appearance to residential structures (fig. 78).

As the towns grew, however, the original rough log and frame structures were either covered over or replaced with the familiar false front of western architecture (fig. 79). False fronts first appeared in great numbers in the California gold rush of 1849. In addition to making a shed look like a two-story building and providing a large surface for the merchant's sign, the fronts gave a citified, more eastern look to a raw frontier town. The tall, long, and narrow shop space behind the one-story false front was entered through a central doorway, flanked by large show windows (figs. 80–82). As the form expanded vertically to two floors, long, narrow windows provided light and air to the living quarters and offices above (fig. 83). A rare three-story false front can be found in Crested Butte (fig. 84). Although slight variations appear, facade doorways are usually central, square or angled, and indented, with overlights and large display windows on each side. The high glass fronts allow maximum light to penetrate the long, narrow buildings. A stairway to the upper floors is usually located to the right or left front (fig. 85). This stairway to the second floor usually ascends

78. An early frame commercial structure, South Park City Museum (Fairplay).

79. A frame false front was added to the log structure of the Miners' Exchange in St. Elmo.

80. A typical one-story commercial false front in Lake City, with central indented entrance flanked by large display windows.

81. Two shops share the common cornice of this commercial false front on the main street of Silver Plume.

82. These typical one-story false fronts in Lake City share a common cornice, forming an early, small business block.

83. Offices and apartments are located above the first-floor shops of these two-story false fronts in Breckenridge. Greek Revival window detailing and contrasting bracketed cornices adorn the facades.

84. A rare three-story false front rises above the main street of Crested Butte.

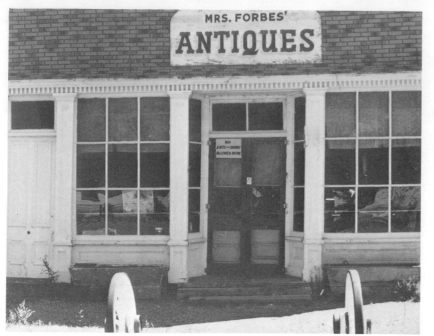

85. This typical arrangement of commercial facade openings, in Lake City, features a central indented doorway flanked by large display windows and access to the second floor at the side.

86. This commercial false front in Crested Butte features unusual cornice treatment as well as an exterior enclosed stairway to the second-floor offices and apartments.

through the interior of the structure; occasionally it appears as a rising, enclosed tunnellike attachment to the side (fig. 86). Interiors of the earlier examples had plank floors and oilcloth walls and ceilings.

The false fronts, having been popular for a long time, were constructed of wood, both log and frame, and later of brick, stone, and iron. Horizontal clapboard siding, vertical board-and-batten siding, and tongue-and-groove siding were popular exterior wood treatments. Stone rubble walls were often used in conjunction with brick fronts. The cast-iron front was less common; it was used most often in Italianate buildings.

An important element of the false-front building is the cornice, which varies from a simple, straight, unadorned finish to decorative treatments of varying heights. Cornices of wood, brick, sheet metal, and cast iron, supported by fanciful brackets and elaborately ornamented, were popular; each attempted to outdo the other in a show of individuality (figs. 87–90). Early, simple cornices were enhanced by the emergence of the gable apex of the roof above the front, creating a triangular pediment at the top (figs. 91, 92). The shape was often adopted without the presence of the roof.

Other than some cornice decoration, detailing was kept very simple. In addition to some Italianate detailing, Greek and Gothic details, which rarely appear in commercial architecture, are occasionally found in the form of pediments and lintels over openings.

Many fine examples of the western false-front style still exist. Many communities never graduated from this mining camp stage of vernacular and false-front structures. The remains of these types of buildings are best found in the less prominent towns, for the more prosperous communities replaced most of their false fronts with more elaborate structures of Italianate and Queen Anne influences.

87. A false front in Silver Plume with typical decorative wood cornice hand-cut by jigsaw.

88. A sheet metal cornice has been attached to this brick false front with a dressed granite surface, in Silver Plume.

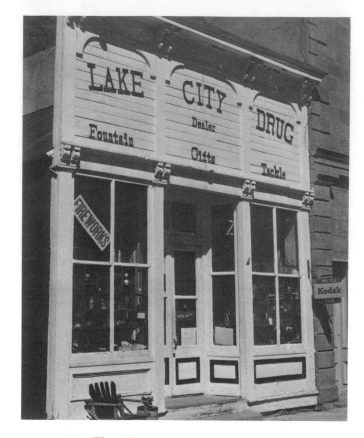

89. The Lake City drugstore features decorative cornices. The surface of the false front provides space for the merchant's advertising.

90. On this wood commercial false front in Silver Plume both intermediate and crowning bracketed cornices top the indented entrance and shop windows.

91. The roof pitch of Heg's Place in Crested Butte becomes an important element as the false front and cornice follow the line of the emerging roof peak.

92. The roof apex of another commercial structure in Crested Butte merges with the false front, creating an interesting cornice line.

ITALIANATE

As a town's wealth increased, the use of the false front to simulate a big-city atmosphere was no longer necessary, as prosperity brought with it the necessary urban qualities. The false front, however, remained an important commercial architectural form in the older, less prominent towns. Other than minor Gothic influences, the first Victorian influence in commercial mining town architecture was Italianate. Eastern architects were already re-creating the elegance of the Italian palazzo, and in the West false fronts were built in emulation of that elegance.

Advances in building technology and transportation, refinement of materials, and availability of funds made the erection of permanent, more substantial buildings like those found in the East possible in these growing frontier mining communities. Although some wood examples exist, buildings constructed of stone, brick, sheet metal, and cast iron were more popular because they were more like the eastern models, created a desired atmosphere of permanence, and offered protection against the ever-present danger of fire.

Most of the Italianate structures had two stories; some had three. The most common floor plan, occasionally varied, follows that of the false front, with a tall, narrow, deep shop or store space on the main level and a central, indented entrance, flanked by large display windows and a door leading to the apartments or offices above (figs. 93, 94). Sometimes, when the first floor has been halved, two adjacent doors at the entranceway lead to the spaces served by the two display windows. Roofs, sealed by asphalt, felt, gravel, and metal, became flat; full upper stories rather than the deceiving empty space were now behind the front. Increased decorative detailing in the Italian tradition appeared in the form of fine ornamental cornices and elaborately detailed windows (figs. 95–99).

The repetition of this form in a sequence of several shops under the same upper floor, cornice, and roof created wider, larger two-story business blocks (figs. 100, 101). These often appeared at intersections with corner, front, and side entrances.

The Italian influence made its most striking appearance in the form of cast-iron fronts (fig. 102). Invented and first erected in New York in 1848, the cast-iron front quickly came into use around the country wherever multistoried commercial buildings were needed. The front's popularity was substantiated by strength, durability, economy, noncombustibility, lightness, resistance to strain, and adaptability to ornament and decoration (figs. 103–6). Unaffected by rapid oxidation, decay, or extreme temperature differences, the front could be disassembled and reerected elsewhere with no injury to any of its parts. The facades could be prepared and fitted in the factory, transported to the site, and put together rapidly in all seasons of the year. They were deliberately made to look like the already accepted wood and stone fronts.

The iron front consists of a row of hollow columns rising uninterruptedly above each other from basement to roof, usually covering a plain brick or stone structure. All the rest of the front is bolted or hangs from these upright pillars with ornamentally

93. This Italianate commercial building in Breckenridge, a rare wood frame example, features decorative window detailing, elaborate cornice, and quoining at the corners.

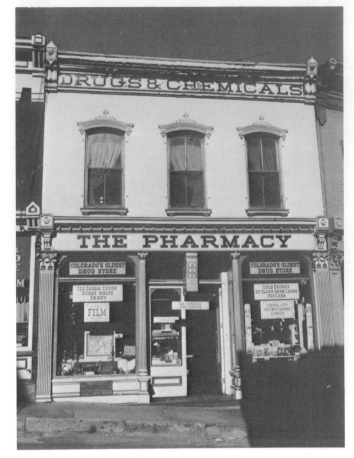

94. The Pharmacy in Central City, built in 1874, is a brick structure displaying decorative metal cornice, window, and column detailing in the Italian tradition.

95. Italian-influenced brick lintels top the segmental arched windows of this commercial building in Silverton.

96. This Italian window detailing of portland cement in Central City features a central keystone.

97

98

97. This window in Lake City is embellished with decorative sheet metal detailing.

98. Italian-influenced sheet metal detailing enhances this window in Central City.

99. Elaborate Italianate metal window and door lintels, varying in design from floor to floor, are found on this brick building in Georgetown. This metal trim was manufactured by the Pullis Brothers of St. Louis, Missouri.

100. Two commercial establishments have been united under the same second-floor facade and bracketed cornice to create this Italianate business block in Silverton. Access to the second floor is through the entrance that separates the shops.

99

100

101

102

101. Three shops under a common second floor form this business block in Black Hawk. Access to second floor is at far right.

102. The first floor of this Italian-influenced commercial building in Telluride is divided by cast-iron piers, which support panels of galvanized iron at the second story.

103. Detail of a cast-iron front in Silverton, cast at the Durango Iron Works.

103

104

105

106

104. Cast-iron detailing on a commercial building, Silverton.

105. Cast-iron detailing on an Italianate commercial building, Central City.

106. Cast-iron detailing on a column in Silverton.

treated nuts (fig. 107). No heavy horizontal courses are necessary on the facade as they are in other kinds of structures, because floor and roof supports rest on the side walls. Only light screens or panelwork unite the uprights. During thunderstorms they act as huge conductors, transferring electricity to the earth.

Often backed by brickwork, the iron holds the bricks in place, and reciprocally, in case of fire, the brickwork protects the iron from direct flames and prevents it from twisting and collapsing. In addition, the brickwork backing serves to equalize the temperature of the building in winter and summer and to keep the interior of the ironwork dry by preventing condensation.

Although the popularity of cast-iron facades diminished in the East in the 1870s, they continued to be widely used in the mining towns as late as the 1880s and in some

107. Decorative metal nuts are often used to bolt cast-iron fronts to brick facades, as in this example from Cripple Creek.

cases into the 1890s. The fronts could be ordered by catalog; many varied designs were available. The most popular mail-order cast-iron facades in Colorado were supplied by the Mesker Brothers of St. Louis, Missouri and Evansville, Indiana, and the Pullis Brothers of St. Louis. Their plaques, identifying themselves as front builders and their companies as architectural ironworks, can still be found at the base of many fronts (figs. 108–10). In addition to these out-of-state manufacturers, Hessell Iron Works of Colorado Springs, Engelbach Brothers of Leadville, Colorado Iron Works in Denver, and Durango Iron Works supplemented the production of iron castings in the state.

In addition to the light, widely spaced structural cast-iron columns on the lower stories, the upper floors were adorned by nonstructural veneers of pressed metal with a varying degree of somewhat Italianate ornamentation which emphasized the plastic

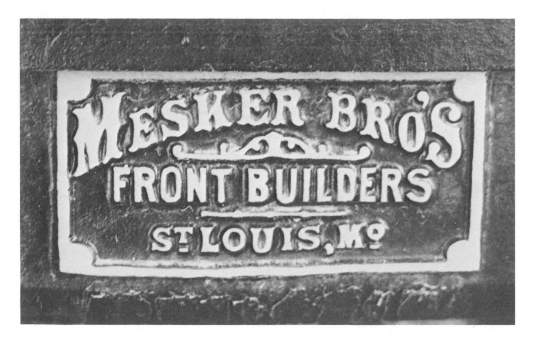

108. Cast-iron fronts often included a plaque displaying the manufacturer's name. This example, in Crested Butte, is one of many Mesker Brothers fronts used in Colorado.

109. Another popular cast-iron front builder advertised on this front in Georgetown.

110. Mesker of Indiana also provided cast-iron fronts for Colorado. This name plate is displayed in Central City.

qualities inherent in the numerous materials used. Window detailing became intricate, with various decorative lintel treatments of cast iron, pressed metal, or composition, and square-headed windows gave way to the Italian segmental head (figs. 95–98). In addition, second-story, square, hexagonal, and octagonal oriel windows were common (figs. 111, 112). Elaborate cornices of wood, brick, and sheet metal were used as crowning elements of varying heights and degrees of complexity and were often placed between floors (figs. 113–17). Quoining at the corners, molded portland cement details, and sheet-metal facing in numerous patterns recalling

111. An octagonal oriel window protrudes from the second story of this wood frame commercial structure in Rico.

112. This beautiful oriel window in Ouray is enhanced by decorative sheet metal detailing.

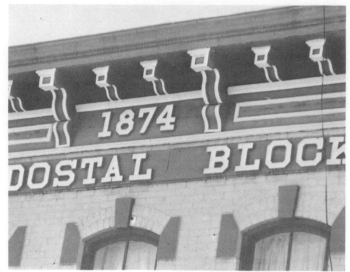

113. This elaborately detailed sheet-metal, bracket-supported cornice crowns a commercial building in Ouray.

114. This metal bracketed cornice and window detailing in Central City exemplify the Italianate influence in commercial architecture.

masonry construction added to the cosmetics of the facade (figs. 118, 119). Ornamentation of the structural tie-rod heads that protruded through the sides of the buildings was common, as was the identification of a business block's owner and construction date in bold letters, both in positions of prominence (figs. 120, 121).

Iron doorsteps and doors with oval glass openings and decorative hardware often lead to interiors that are generally more elaborate than earlier examples (figs. 122–25). Patterned wallpaper, tile floors, decorative wainscoting, and stamped metal ceiling designs provide a pleasant Victorian atmosphere (figs. 126–29).

The Italianate influence, joined by the Queen Anne Panel Brick style, remained popular in the mining communities until the 1890s. Although changes have been made, due to their permanent nature many examples exist today throughout the mining towns and function well, as they did then, as stores, shops, and offices.

115. Lavish metal detailing adorns these commercial facades in Central City.

116

117

116. Varying decorative cornice treatments on two commercial buildings in Ouray.

117. Different adjoining cornice treatments in Georgetown.

118. Brick quoining at the corners of this Italianate commercial structure in Black Hawk gives the appearance of more massive stone construction.

119. In an effort to represent stone construction, stamped metal panels of this type were often used to cover commercial facades.

118

119

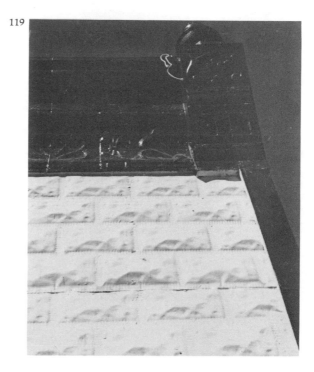

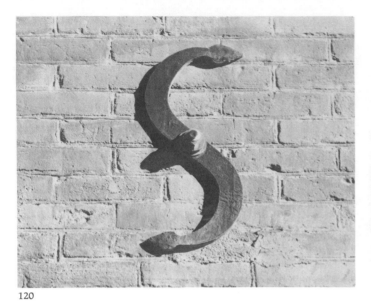

120

121

120. The heads of structural tie rods, protruding from wall surfaces, are often treated decoratively, as in this example from Central City.

121. The name of the founder and financial backer of a business block often appears on a commercial facade with the date of construction. Hyman Block is in Leadville.

122. This fine commercial entrance is in Cripple Creek.

123. Elaborately detailed door handles often enhanced commercial entrances.

124. Patterned iron footplates like this one in Silver Plume are often located at commercial entrances.

122

123

124

125

126

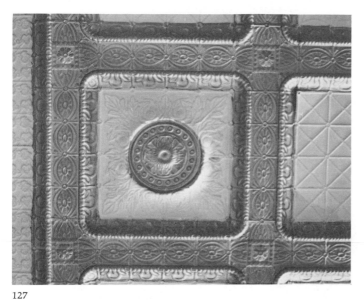

127

125. Brass hardware was often used decoratively. This hinge is on a bank door in the South Park City Museum (Fairplay).

126. Tile floors like this example in Silverton brighten many commercial interiors.

127. Stamped sheet metal patterns like this beautiful example in Cripple Creek often adorn the walls and ceilings of commercial establishments.

128. Wood paneling in a Victor commercial building.

129. Stamped metal ceilings were often complex, as seen in this example from a Telluride commercial structure.

128

129

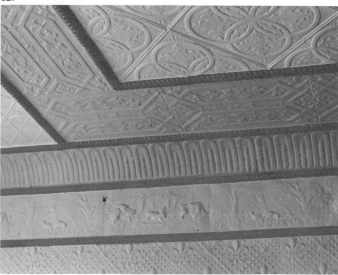

QUEEN ANNE

Queen Anne–style commercial buildings, unlike residential buildings in this style, made great use of Panel Brick decoration. These facades, constructed of pressed brick laid with thin, precise mortar joints, were present in the mining communities in the 1880s and 1890s, when Italianate commercial structures were popular. Queen Anne buildings differed from the earlier forms only in the character of surface decoration; the floor plans remained generally the same: shops and stores on the first floor and offices and living quarters above. Combinations of the Italianate and Queen Anne styles often occurred, while sometimes the Queen Anne broke away from the use of cast iron and sheet metal, using only brick to animate the surface. Growing out of Greek Revival brickwork, where dentil courses and entablatures were suggested with the use of common brick, the style is characterized by projecting and receding panels of intricate brickwork designs (figs. 130–39). As Bunting points out, "Being formed of common brick, this decoration is an integral part of the masonry fabric of the building and its scale and character stem from the material itself."[6] Many exterior treatments overlapped with the Romanesque Revival which followed.

Many examples of this style continue to function today in the mining towns, especially in towns which were rebuilt after fires. Cripple Creek, destroyed by fire in 1896, rebuilt to a large degree in this style and has the best remaining examples.

130. This brick-facaded stone commercial building in Russell Gulch displays simple Queen Anne brickwork at the cornice.

131

132

131. The second story of this commercial building in Silverton combines Queen Anne brickwork with an oriel window and Italian segmental arch windows.

132. Queen Anne string courses connect the windows on this commercial building in Leadville. String courses tie the building together visually and aid in animating the surface.

133. Queen Anne brickwork can be very intricate, as illustrated in this example from Leadville.

134. This elaborate brickwork in Georgetown is capped by a stamped sheet metal cornice, merging Italian and Queen Anne influences.

135. Decorative Queen Anne brickwork on a Georgetown commercial building.

133

134   135

136. Queen Anne brickwork animates the face of this commercial structure in Durango.

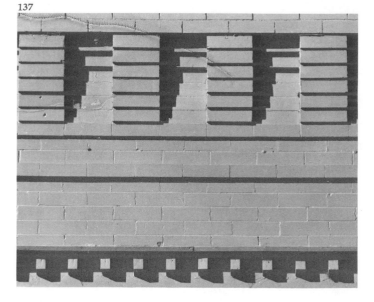

137. Decorative brick detailing on a Cripple Creek commercial building.

138. This Queen Anne brickwork in Leadville includes treatment reminiscent of Greek dentil courses.

139. Decorative Queen Anne brickwork on a Cripple Creek commercial building.

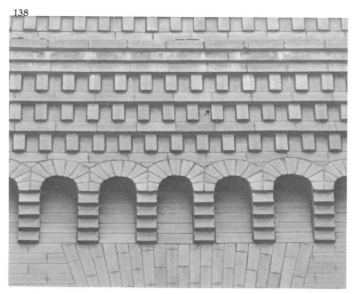

Romanesque Revival

Like the Italianate and Queen Anne influences, the Romanesque Revival made a strong imprint on commercial architecture in the eighties and nineties. Often blending with Queen Anne brickwork, the round-arched Richardsonian window opening, sometimes with archivolts, was a common second-story treatment (figs. 140–45).

The monumental, fortresslike Richardsonian Romanesque style was most often used for banks in the more prosperous towns. Two- and three-story buildings in Durango, Telluride, and Leadville, originally banks with apartments and offices on the floors above, are good examples of this style with the characteristic rusticated, rough-textured masonry wall surfaces of sandstone, medieval towers, and heavy, round, rock-faced arches (figs. 146–49).

Colonial Revival

Because the Colonial Revival arrived late in the mining communities, around the turn of the century, it had little influence on the commercial structures. Effects of the revival were felt in some of the later communities of the town phase of development with the appearance of classic detailing on earlier Victorian forms (figs. 150–53).

140. The round-arched windows of Romanesque Revival join Queen Anne brickwork on this commercial structure in Silverton.

141. This business block in Ouray combines characteristic Queen Anne brickwork with Romanesque window detailing.

142. Romanesque round-arched windows and Queen Anne brickwork are combined on the face of this commercial building in Cripple Creek.

143. This fine example of the merging of Queen Anne and Romanesque detailing is in Durango. The presence of archivolts over the windows is a common Romanesque feature.

144. Combined Queen Anne and Romanesque features adorn the facade of this business block in Ouray.

145. Merging Queen Anne and Romanesque elements animate this Cripple Creek commercial facade.

146. This heavy rusticated sandstone structure in Telluride exemplifies the influence of Romanesque Revival in commercial architecture. The building was originally a bank, its entrance capped by a characteristic tower.

147. This rock-faced, round-arched Richardsonian commercial building is in Silverton.

148. This three-story Romanesque Revival bank in Leadville is topped by a tower, a familiar feature of the style.

149. Its impregnable appearance made the Romanesque Revival popular in bank architecture. This rough-faced example is in Durango.

150. Such Colonial Revival features as swags and classic columns appeared near the turn of the century. This commercial example is in Cripple Creek.

151. Colonial detailing of pressed metal adorns this commercial building in Victor, photographed during a snowstorm. The use of leaded glass was a popular holdover from earlier styles.

152. Colonial swags and columns of stamped sheet metal have been added to this commercial structure in Cripple Creek.

153. Colonial features are best represented in later towns like Cripple Creek and Victor, which rebuilt after fires in the late 1890s. This commercial example is in Cripple Creek.

Transportation

Transportation, both for the ore and for the miners, was essential. Feet, skis, and snowshoes were indispensable, and most of the early explorations were carried out with the help of a burro or a mule. Mules were strung out and roped together in pack-trains, with one man riding the lead animal and another at the rear. Burros, on the other hand, were allowed to travel loose and were driven only from behind, as they were quite intelligent and could be trusted to march single file when the trail was narrow. The packtrains could carry great quantities of supplies and were often guided by dogs.

From the valley towns, roads were built to the mining camps. Toll road companies, which built roads and bridges, were formed. The tolls collected provided the funds for improvements and for new roads. Though very narrow and steep, these pioneer roads were better than the pack trails and enabled wagons of supplies to reach all but the most inaccessible camps.

Wherever there were people, there were ten times as many head of stock, so barns, corrals, livery stables, and blacksmith shops had to be built. Simple private log and frame barns were constructed near the residences. Usually one and one-half stories, with a large open space for horses and wagons and a loft area above for hay storage, the barns had a large, wide, central entrance, often with a rolling door, a hay opening in the gable above with a hoist, and a pitched roof (fig. 154). A few of the fancier homes had more elaborate barns.

Livery stables and blacksmith shops were laid out like barns, with large, open

154. An old plank-sided barn in Breckenridge with a characteristic hay opening above the main entrance.

lower-level spaces and haylofts above. Blacksmith shops, where horses were shod and wagons repaired, were closely associated with the livery stables, usually either under the same roof or next door (fig. 155). Livery stables rented horses and carriages and provided overnight quarters for the horses and carriages of visitors. An Idaho Springs livery stable charged $2.50 per day for saddle horses and $10.00 for a double team with their carriage. Livery stables were built like barns but, because of their public function, added familiar commercial qualities to their facades. The wooden false front was most common, and more decorative brick and stone examples occasionally appeared (figs. 156–59).

Where there were no trains, stagecoaches carried mail and passengers. Drawn by four to six mules or horses in pairs, the coaches reached speeds of four to five miles per hour. On steep grades, logs were sometimes dragged along as brakes; the leather straps used for suspension allowed the coach to swing from side to side, creating quite a rough ride. Carrying passengers, mail, and light freight, the coaches made frequent stops at relay stations, where the animals, having been kept at a steady gallop, were changed. Stagecoaches to Leadville sometimes had as many as nine people crammed inside and four or five riding on top. Some coaches had iron shutters as protection against Indians and road agents (highwaymen), and firearms were handed out if the passengers requested them.

Freighting outfits, which aided in the transportation of ore and supplies, used oxen, mules, and horses. They maintained huge corrals where the freight wagons were stationed and the stock cared for. Six to eight mules per freight wagon were used for normal loads, while oxen—as many as twenty on one wagon, making ten miles a day—were used for heavy loads. One mountain freighting business employed over two thousand mules and horses hauling goods to and from Leadville before the advent of the railroad. The animals caused traffic problems and pollution: "Freight teams blocked sidewalks and streets, littering the area with manure and straw much to the discomfort of those who had to wade through the resulting mess and confusion."[7]

155. The old false-fronted wood blacksmith shop in Ouray.

156. An early false-fronted livery stable in Brecken-ridge.

157. This early livery stable in Ouray, built in 1883, has the usual hay door above the large, central entrance.

158. This livery stable in Leadville features a magnificent wood front with false windows and Greek pediments over the central entrance and hay opening above.

159. Decorated with simple Queen Anne brickwork at the cornice, this stone livery stable in Black Hawk has a brick facade.

The appearance of the railroad made a greater impact on the mining towns than any other factor in their development. A much more efficient mode of transportation than the earlier packtrains, wagons, and poorly kept toll roads, railroads were used to take ore out, bring supplies in, and transport people. Many engineering feats were accomplished in building tunnels and trestles through difficult, mountainous terrain. As Lucius Beebe reports:

> The grade is very steep in some places exceeding two hundred feet to the mile for short distances. The difficulty of surmounting it is greatly augmented by the almost constant curvature of the track. Very little is straight. Reverse curves succeed one another as continuous as the track of a snake.[8]

In addition to snowslides, floods, rockslides, and other violent natural acts, accidents such as train wrecks, boiler explosions, runaways, and derailments were common.
Beebe also comments:

> The dominant characteristic of almost all Colorado railroading in the nineteenth century, like that of all the enterprises of the era, was one of speculation, bonanza, and impermanence. In an age when silver was commonly used for pavements, barber shop floors, and the humblest household utensils and appointments, thousands upon thousands of miles of railroad, both narrow-gage and standard gage, were projected, never in fact to operate. At one time there were so many railroads running into the boom town of Leadville that a traveler had a choice of four different approaches.[9]

Aspen, with a population of eleven thousand, had ten passenger trains daily in 1893, and fifty-eight trains per day ran between Cripple Creek and Victor.

Train travel in the early railroading days of the Rockies was informal. Hard wooden seats with no padding, crowded cars, and slow speeds made for unpleasant travel conditions. The simple cars gave way to "palace cars" with velvet seats, lavish Pullman cars, and elegant buffet dining cars. The coaches were thirty-five feet long and seven feet wide, with single and double red plush seats for thirty-six passengers on either side of a seventeen-inch aisle. Lit by clerestory windows, the coaches also had oil lamps hanging from the ceiling and coal stoves for heat. The three-hour ride from Denver to Central City cost $3.10; the journey from Denver to Georgetown cost $4.30. Describing early passenger service into Creede, one observer wrote, "The train, when it comes into sight, is a sight to behold. Men sit on each other and on the arms of seats, stand in the aisles, and hang on the platforms."[10]

The Victorian train depot, a place of glamour and excitement, was designed to look the part. It was the center of the community and the only reliable link to the outside world, as most roads were blocked by snow and mud for months. Tents along the tracks sometimes served as a station until the depot was built, and at Creede, a boxcar served as an early ticket office. The railroad depot evolved a uniquely functional style of its own. The long, narrow structures stretch along the tracks. They are characterized by a hip or pitched roof with a sweeping bracket-supported overhang reminiscent of the Italian influence. The overhang sheltered passengers on the platform and made it unnecessary to build pillars, which might get in the way of opening train doors. Although most depots were constructed of wood with clapboard, tongue-and-groove, or board-and-batten siding, an occasional brick or stone example can be found; one is the Cripple Creek station, which also differs from the norm by having a third floor (figs. 160–63). The more common one- and two-story depots include, on the first level, large, open passenger waiting areas, freight and baggage storage areas, a ticket office, and a control room with a characteristic bay window for clear viewing of the tracks. The second floor, when present, usually served as the stationmaster's quarters. Wainscoting is common both inside and out to protect the walls against baggage cart collisions, and a yellow and brown color scheme is traditional. Large, open structures of similar style served as freight depots.

Excellent examples of railroad depots, many still in use, exist in a great number of the mining communities. A roundhouse still used for engine storage can be found in Durango.

Food and Lodging

Since sleeping accommodations were often hard to come by in the early mining settlements, the bedroll was an important part of every man's equipment. Large tents often provided the only adequate shelter. In Leadville, according to one account,

The first arrivals found plenty of company, but few accommodations. A huge tent was hastily constructed in the fall of 1878 to accommodate

160. With its sweeping roof overhang and exterior wainscot protection, the railroad station in Wagon Wheel Gap is a typical Victorian depot. The station-master's quarters are above the first-floor waiting area, ticket office, and control room.

161. This long depot stretches along the tracks at Creede. Exterior surfaces include wainscoting and vertical board-and-batten siding.

162. The more elaborate Victor depot, built of brick in 1895, includes a hip roof and an unusual treatment of the characteristic bay window.

163. Built on a sloping site, the three-story brick and stone station in Cripple Creek features a two-story bay window for observing the tracks, a waiting room at the second-floor track level, and a first-floor street entrance on the opposite side of the depot.

political meetings and later was provided with three tiers of bunks with calico curtains, in which 1000 men could sleep—and thus yield the owner a thousand dollars a night.[11]

An early arrival in Pueblo wrote:

> Father and I rented cots our first night in Pueblo. When a thousand-odd men began snoring in unison the din was horrible. Added to that, the place literally crawled with bedbugs. After tossing and tumbling sleeplessly all night, we decided to get our rest under the pale stars.[12]

An early lodging house in Pitkin was described as a large tent, eighteen by fifty feet, with a floor of sawdust-covered ground and canvas partitions separating the sleeping compartments. In addition to a stove, trunks, and boxes, other furnishings consisted of two tiers of bunks, one above the other, made of rough boards and arranged in a row at the sides of the room. George Pullman, who developed the Pullman car, claimed that his idea came from such early mining bunk arrangements. At first people slept on loose hay; later, feather mattresses were used. Coats did duty as pillows. The going price for such accommodations was fifty cents to a dollar a night.

Log lodging houses, stagecoach inns, and miners' boardinghouses soon joined the tent accommodations. Although similar in construction to previously discussed log buildings, they served a different function, and their shape reflected it. A description of the Denver House, the leading hotel in 1859 Denver, will show its differences from the smaller residential and commercial log examples:

> [It] was about 60 feet long and 30 wide. Its four sides consisted of roughly hewn logs. It had a slanting, skeleton roof, covered with canvas. In the interior were neither floors nor ceilings nor walls, nor solid partitions to divide the space; but canvas nailed on frames served to set it off for different purposes to the height of 7 feet. The front part was occupied by a bar for the sale of strong drinks only, and a dozen gambling tables. . . . Next to the barroom came another space enclosed by canvas partitions where the meals were served. Immediately behind it six apartments for sleeping purposes, divided only by the same light material, were set off on each side of a passage. . . . There was no furniture but the gambling and other tables and benches and chairs, made out of rough boards. Bedsteads were provided of the same material, without mattress or pillows, and also tin wash basins, which the guests themselves filled out of barrels of water standing in the passageway, and emptied, after use, on the dirt floor.[13]

A fine two-and-one-half-story, twenty-five-room log miners' hotel, built in 1872, still remains in Gold Hill (fig. 164).

Because they were built early in remote locations, stagecoach inns, which provided resting places for weary travelers, were usually constructed of logs. Most had two stories; layouts included a kitchen space and dining and gathering area on the

164. The old two-and-one-half-story log miners' hotel in Gold Hill was built in 1872.

first floor and second-story dormitory spaces. Corrals were often built nearby for resting horses. Good examples of these early log lodging structures remain. The Mill City House in Dumont was built along the early Clear Creek toll road in the 1860s and once entertained General Grant on a trip to Idaho Springs. Constructed of rough square-hewn logs, with crude wood floors, it had the first saloon west of Denver (fig. 165). The Mosquito Pass Stagecoach Inn, now in South Park City, operated in the 1880s.

Hotels sprang up in great numbers; Creede once had over one hundred. Construction and style advanced as the communities grew and developed. Although not as common as it was in stores and offices, the false front made some appearances on early frame hotel buildings. The simple false-front treatment of the old main street hotel of Silver Plume was typical. Hotels usually had a main-floor lobby and second-floor rooms; unlike shops and offices, they added a porch to the front and a balcony above with second-floor access (fig. 166). An example of more elaborate false-fronted hotel architecture can be found in Ouray. The large, three-story Western Hotel, built in 1890, features a profusion of decorative wood detailing, including carved porch columns, balcony balustrade, and bracketed cornice (fig. 167). Three main doors lead to a large first floor with lobby, dining area, two bars, and a central staircase leading to the rooms above.

In the more prosperous towns, hotel architecture became as lavish as that of residences and stores. Many of the two- and three-story structures used the popular Italian detailing that embellished the commercial structures around them (fig. 168). Walk-up hotels, often resembling the business architecture around them, were common; the lobby and rooms were above shops and stores (figs. 169–71). Larger, more independent hotels with Italian-influenced detailing and some Queen Anne brickwork appeared, sometimes with as many as three stories of rooms above first-floor lobbies, restaurants, and bars. In the more prosperous towns, however, the hotel architecture was most greatly influenced by the grandeur and elegance of French

165. The log Mill City House in Dumont was built in the 1860s as a stage stop along an early Clear Creek toll road.

166. Unlike false-fronted stores, this old wood frame hotel in Silver Plume features a porch and a second-floor balcony.

167. The three-story wood frame Western Hotel in Ouray, built in 1890, includes elaborate wood detailing.

168. Simple Italianate and Queen Anne detailing adorn the brick Gilpin Hotel in Black Hawk.

169. The entrance to the Antlers Hotel in Victor advertises the low prices of an earlier time.

170. A typical ground-floor entrance and stairway leading to the second-floor lobby of a walk-up hotel in Leadville.

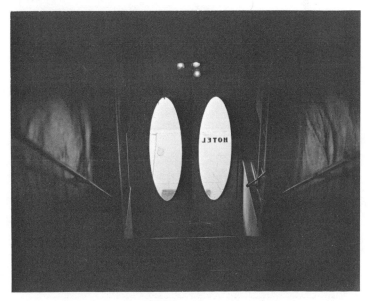

171. The Delaware Block in Leadville includes ground-floor commercial shops with second- and third-floor lobby and rooms. Italianate window detailing merges with the French influence and simple Queen Anne brickwork on the exterior of the walk-up hotel.

châteaus and palaces (figs. 172–74). The French influence, which was felt more in hotel design than any other type of architecture, was translated through the use of wood, brick, stone, sheet metal, and cast iron. The large three- and four-story structures, often with fifty to one hundred rooms, are characterized by mansard roofs, dormer windows, and elaborate exterior detailing in the form of molded portland-cement lintels, sculptural decorations, and carved stone reliefs. The elegant interiors usually include tall ceilings, wide hallways, elaborate staircases, fine furnishings, and central courtyards (figs. 175, 176). Early indoor plumbing facilities were rather primitive. In the Strater Hotel in Durango, the restrooms on each floor actually formed a two-story privy, requiring strategic placement of the holes and shafts leading into the wooden sewer below. Rooms costing from two to four dollars per night, with individual stoves for heat and washbasins with water pitchers, gave way to more elaborate surroundings in places like the Hotel de Paris in Georgetown (figs. 177–79).

> The hotel was luxuriously comfortable with steam heat, hot and cold running water in each room, marble lavatory bowls, corner mirrors, the finest Wilton carpet, gas lights, black walnut furniture, carved and decorated by the master hand of François Gallet, the aged French Cabinetmaker of Georgetown.[14]

One early restaurant, a sixteen-by-twenty-four-foot tent with sawdust floors, served a breakfast of steak, bacon, eggs, hash browns, corn bread, biscuits, butter, and coffee for fifty cents. The staple foods in the mining communities were meat and potatoes, with baked goods such as bread and cakes on the side. In addition to first-floor restaurants in commercial buildings, food stands were common in the streets. Most hotels had restaurants that prepared lavish meals for hotel guests and townspeople alike (fig. 180). Many hotels had fenced areas for poultry and greenhouses or gardens for vegetables. An elaborate New Year's dinner given at the

172. The mansard-capped Central Hotel in Durango was built in the 1880s. Commercial establishments are located on the first floor, hotel lobby and rooms above.

173. The Vendome Hotel (Tabor Grande Hotel), built in Leadville by bonanza king Horace Tabor in the 1880s, is an elaborate example of French grandeur in a mining community. The hotel still provides comfortable accommodations.

Teller House in Central City in 1872 offered fish, beef, veal, mutton, pork, turkey, oysters, duck, grouse, prairie chicken, wild turkey, antelope, venison, bear, buffalo, vegetables, relishes, side dishes, pastries, puddings, ice cream, and jellies for five dollars.[15]

Many original hotels can still be found in the mining towns. Several are still in business, offering fine food and lodging accommodations.

174. The French-influenced Beaumont Hotel in Ouray was built in 1886. Multiple facades are used in an effort to create the appearance of a townscape.

175. A steam radiator, reception desk, and staircase dominate the lobby of the Vendome Hotel (Tabor Grande Hotel) in Leadville.

176. The main staircase of the lavish Teller House, now a Central City museum, ascends from the lobby to the comfortable rooms above.

177. This opulent sitting room in the Hotel de Paris, Georgetown, currently a museum, includes a fireplace and comfortable leather furniture.

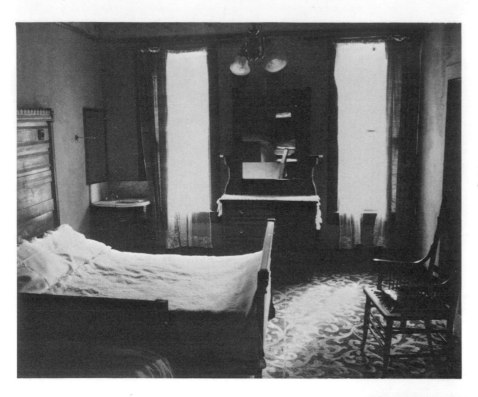

178. A fine bedroom in the Hotel de Paris, Georgetown.

179. A smaller, less elaborate room in the Vendome Hotel (Tabor Grande Hotel), Leadville.

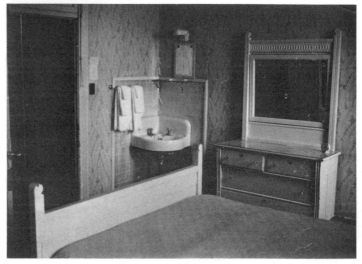

180. The Hotel de Paris in Georgetown, built between 1875 and 1890, offered fine dining accommodations.

Entertainment

SALOONS, GAMBLING HALLS, AND PARLOR HOUSES

The activities centered in the red-light district provided the most popular forms of entertainment for the miners in every town. When miners struck it rich they had the attitude of easy come, easy go. No one seemed to care about the high prices, and many were broke in a short time. In the Cripple Creek and Victor area much of the $432,974,848 which was brought out of the district's 475 mines in less than fifteen years was spent in saloons or brothels, commonly known as parlor houses.

Saloons, among the earliest business establishments to appear in the mining communities, followed the usual tent, log, and frame sequence of construction. The bar was often a board resting on kegs. Frequently associated with gambling and prostitution, saloons were also located in nearly every hotel and in many familiar commercial structures, on the first floor (figs. 181, 182). Gambling generally went on in most saloons and sporting houses, and in the back rooms of major hotels. Popular games were keno, faro, poker, and roulette. Many saloons offered free drinks to gamblers and some provided a free funeral to anyone killed on the premises. The interior and exterior architectural treatment of saloons resembled that of commercial shops and stores. The large, open space of a saloon, which initially had wood floors and oilcloth walls, was often decorated later with tile floors, patterned stamped-metal ceilings, elaborate wood wainscoting and—the center of attraction—a lavish, hand-carved wood bar, usually from Europe (figs. 183–88). Saloons were extremely profitable, as indicated by their popularity in Leadville: "Nearly a hundred licensed

181. Rachel's Place, an early false-fronted frame saloon, originally located in Alma, is now in the South Park City Museum (Fairplay). A decorative bracketed cornice crowns the front.

182. The Pick and Gad, one of the most notorious sporting houses in Telluride, offered drinking and gambling on the first floor and girls on the second. A simple Queen Anne brickwork cornice embellishes the facade.

183. The large open space of Rachel's Place in South Park City includes wood floors and wainscoting, patterned wallpaper, and period furnishings.

184. Also in Rachel's Place is a large, elaborately carved bar. Most bars were made in Europe and shipped to the United States, where they became a standard feature of western saloons.

185. The Sheridan Hotel bar in Telluride, still active today, offers pleasant Victorian surroundings with wood floors and a handsome carved bar.

186. Decorative tile floors like this Cripple Creek example were common in saloons.

187. Stamped sheet metal, intricately detailed, was popular as a covering for saloon walls and ceilings. This panel is found in Leadville.

188. This decorative pressed sheet metal panel comes from a Cripple Creek saloon.

saloons and a dozen gambling houses were in full blast day and night—the largest in the state, situated on Chestnut Street, averaging profits of $32,000 a month."[16]

Prostitutes worked out of structures ranging from simple one- and two-room shacks called cribs to elaborate two-story parlor houses which provided food, liquor, and entertainment. Unpainted pine cribs ran for a quarter of a mile in Cripple Creek, housing French, Japanese, Chinese, Mexican, Indian, and Negro girls. The flimsy frame affairs fronted on the street with a narrow door and tiny window (fig. 189). Girls with two rooms entertained in the front while the back served as a kitchen. Furnishings consisted of an iron bed, straight chairs, and a stove. Often the cribs were the end of the line for former parlor-house girls, who died there of disease, liquor and other drugs, or suicide, as described in this vivid account:

> The room, it is said, is only a sample of the rest on the ricketty [sic] old row. The walls and ceiling were absolutely black with smoke and dirt, excepting where old, stained newspapers had been pasted on them—on the ceiling, to exclude rain and melting snow, and on the walls, to cover up spots from which the plastering had fallen. The floor was rickety and filthy. Around the walls were disposed innumerable unwashed and battered tin cooking utensils, shelves, for the most part laden with dust, old clothing, which emitted a powerful effluvium, hung from nails here and there; or tumble-down chairs, a table of very rheumatic tendency, on which were broken cups, plates and remnants of food, were scattered all over its surface. An empty whiskey bottle and pewter spoon or two. In one corner and taking up half the space of the den was the bedstead strongly suggestive of a bountiful

189. These small, Gothic-detailed wood frame structures in Telluride are among the few cribs still standing.

crop of vermin, and on that flimsy bed lay the corpse of the suicide, clad in dirty ragged apparel, and with as horrid a look on her begrimmed, pallid features as the surroundings presented.[17]

Although many girls entertained men in rooms available over saloons and elsewhere, as well as in the modest cribs, the most successful prostitutes worked in fancy parlor houses with reception rooms, gambling rooms, bars, banquet rooms, and individual rooms upstairs with brass beds. A building that once housed this swank type of parlor house can still be found in Cripple Creek. The posh Homestead Parlor House on Myers Avenue, once the center of the city's red-light district, was reconstructed of brick after the original wood building burned down in 1896 (fig 190). The two-story structure with Colonial Revival detailing housed five to six girls plus a staff of seven. Gambling tables and saloon were downstairs and girls' rooms upstairs, with individual coal stoves; the house also had electric lights, running water, telephone, and intercom. Customers could look through a hallway window on the second floor to choose their companions. Opium dens or "hop joints" were also popular in the red-light districts, and prostitutes were often addicts.

Red-light districts were commonly located in undesirable parts of town, usually near the railroad tracks. Other than the saloons located in hotels and in main-street commercial buildings, few examples of these building types remain. Fire has destroyed what were predominantly wood frame structures.

190. The Homestead Parlor House in Cripple Creek offered drinking and gambling on the first floor with girls' rooms on the second. The Colonial Revival detailing reflects its late construction date.

CLUBS AND FRATERNAL ORGANIZATIONS

Social and business clubs were masculine refuges from the trials and tribulations of family life. Nearly every man belonged to one or another of the many fraternal organizations. Although some clubs prohibited females, others had their own women's groups. The laws governing the clubs were quite strict, often prohibiting gambling.

Many of these clubs were located on the second floors of commercial blocks, over stores and shops. Some such blocks display the club's name or symbol on the facade. Large buildings of varying styles with several meeting halls and rooms occasionally represent the fraternities, as exemplified by the two-story Colonial Revival Masonic Hall in Victor and the two-story French-influenced Elks Club in Ouray (figs. 191, 192).

Popular clubs and organizations in the mining communities included Elks, Masons, Odd Fellows, Knights of Pythias, Good Templars, Order of the Eastern Star, Woodmen of the World, Women of Woodcraft, Caledonian Club, the Rathbone Sisters, Fraternal Order of Eagles, and several miners' clubs and unions. Many organizations continue to use their original meeting places.

THEATERS AND OPERA HOUSES

Traveling minstrel shows and vaudeville companies made one-night stands in many towns. Some early theaters charged no admission and made their money on drinks sold at the bar. Sometimes a billiard hall was attached. One early theater in 1860 was described as follows:

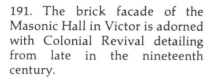

191. The brick facade of the Masonic Hall in Victor is adorned with Colonial Revival detailing from late in the nineteenth century.

192. The unique brick facade of the Ouray Elks Club, built in 1904, combines French, Queen Anne, and Romanesque influences.

Denver already boasted the Apollo Theater, neither ceiled, nor plastered, illuminated by twelve candles and containing rough benches for 350 people. As it was the upper story of a popular drinking saloon, clinking glasses, rattling billiard balls, and uproarious songs interfered with the performance. The price of admission was one dollar. . . . Among the spectators were several ladies, and despite the boisterousness of the house there was no gross coarseness and no profanity.[18]

Few of the theaters remain. A one-story, wooden, false-front structure in Telluride exemplifies a small theater of the time, with one big room and a shallow stage at one end (fig. 193). Chairs were rarely fastened down in early theaters, as the large open space might also serve the community as schoolroom, dance hall, or meeting place.

Opera houses gained their greatest popularity in the more prosperous towns. The large, elegant structures provided the best stage entertainment available in the country. The two-story Central City Opera House, built in 1878, features a modified mansard roof, Richardsonian arched openings and rough masonry face, and second-story musicians' balcony (fig. 194). The 750-seat interior is elaborately decorated with murals and contains handmade hickory chairs and a central chandelier. The candles that originally lit the stage were later replaced with gas footlights. The Central City Opera House is still in use today.

Although the interior of the Ouray opera house, Wrights Hall, has been changed, the exterior offers a magnificent example of a cast-iron front, the ultimate in Mesker Brothers mail-order designs (figs. 195, 196).

The Aspen Opera House offered boxes upholstered in plush, with brass trimmings. The walls were treated with ornamental woodwork, decorative paper, and frescoes. Twelve scenery sets and twelve dressing rooms were additional features.

The Tabor Opera House in Leadville was built in 100 days in 1879 (fig. 197). The

110

193. The interior of this simple wood frame false-fronted theater in Telluride consists of a large, open seating area with a shallow stage at the rear.

194. The facade of the 750-seat Central City Opera House, which opened in 1878, is treated with Romanesque detailing capped by a modified mansard roof with bull's-eye window. A musicians' balcony cantilevers above the entrance.

exterior of the three-story brick structure is adorned with Italian detailing of molded portland cement. The foyer has a cashier's cage; a private suite and offices for the Tabor family occupy the floors above. The 800-seat interior includes 400 main-floor and 400 balcony seats of cast iron and plush (fig. 198). Canvas flats and drops provided scenery; the dressing rooms were beneath the stage. The Tabor Opera House is now a museum.

195. Wrights Hall, the opera house of Ouray, sports one of the most magnificent Mesker Brothers metal fronts. Cast-iron piers at the first floor support the pressed metal veneer of the second story. The building no longer functions as an opera house.

196. Exuberant galvanized iron detailing on Wrights Hall, Ouray.

197. The three story brick Tabor Opera House in Leadville opened in 1879. Portland cement lintels, cast on the site, cap the windows. A Greek pediment at the cornice tops the facade.

198. Now a museum, the Tabor Opera House includes 400 main-floor seats and another 400 in the curved balcony. This photo shows the stage set with original backdrops.

Other Forms of Entertainment

Other popular forms of entertainment included picnics, dancing, band concerts (fig. 199), chamber music, circuses, parades, lectures, and church suppers. Baseball was popular, and local merchants often sponsored teams as a good means of advertising. Other common activities were hose-cart racing among firehouse teams, roller skating, boxing matches, wrestling matches, and rock drilling contests among the miners.

199. The old bandstand in Silver Plume was the center of popular musical entertainment.

These matches of both one- and two-man teams often drew large purses. One member of a two-man team held and turned the drill while the other struck blows with an eight-pound jackhammer. In addition, a racetrack at Gillett offered horse races, rodeos, and, on one occasion, a bullfight. The town of Cameron, near Cripple Creek, attracted visitors from all over the district with a small zoo and amusement park.

Winter activities included ice skating, sledding, skiing, showshoeing, and tobogganing. During the winter of 1896, the Ice Palace, a pseudo-Norman castle, was constructed on five acres in Leadville, entirely of blocks of ice. The walls were 8 feet thick, and the towers alone contained 5,000 tons of ice. Entering the north gateway after paying fifty cents admission, the visitor followed a grand stairway to an ice rink, 80 by 190 feet. The palace also had a ballroom, an auxiliary ballroom, and a dining room. Exhibits were frozen in the walls, ice pillars supported the roof, and coal heaters provided the warmth for skaters and dancers. The structure melted in the spring of the same year.

Another social activity was joining the National Guard or military companies, whose armories became popular social gathering places. Many people also visited health spas and hot springs like those at Idaho Springs and Glenwood Springs. Camping and watching wild animals rounded out the numerous forms of recreation available in mining towns.

6
Institutional Architecture

County Courthouses

Found only in towns which had been selected as county seats, county courthouses are usually monumental two-story structures situated in prominent locations. Although most examples are constructed of stone and brick, the Hinsdale County Courthouse (1877) in Lake City is wood, as is the Clear Creek County Courthouse (1868) in Georgetown. The structures generally have similar interior plans but vary in external appearance depending on which architectural influence was popular at the time of their construction. From the simple frame courthouse in Lake City, later examples were influenced by more elaborate French, Italianate, and Romanesque styles. Courthouses in these styles are found in Ouray (Ouray County, 1888), Central City (Gilpin County, 1904), and Rico (Dolores County) (figs. 200–203). Colonial Revival courthouses followed; good examples can be seen in Cripple Creek (Teller County, 1904) and Silverton (San Juan County, 1906) (figs. 204, 205).

County offices on the first floor usually flank a central hallway or open space, and stairways, often at both ends of the building, lead to second-story courtrooms (figs. 206, 207). As in most public buildings, interior wainscoting was a popular feature, and elaborate woodwork was common. An exception to the usual square and rectangular plans, the San Juan County Courthouse follows a cruciform arrangement. The jail is usually near the courthouse or inside, as in the San Miguel County Courthouse in Telluride, where a number of cells are located on the first floor of the building.

116

200. Still in use today, the simple wood frame Hinsdale County Courthouse in Lake City was built in 1877. County offices occupy the first floor, courtrooms the second.

201. Towers and cupolas were popular external elements on courthouses. This mansard-capped cupola is on the Ouray County Court-house, built in 1888.

202. Italian towers and Roman-esque arches dominate Central City's Gilpin County Courthouse, built in 1904.

203. The Dolores County Courthouse in Rico reflects Romanesque influence.

204. Built in 1904, the Teller County Courthouse in Cripple Creek, with Colonial and later Georgian Revival–influenced exterior, houses the standard first-floor offices and second-floor courtrooms.

205. In contrast to earlier examples, the San Juan County Courthouse in Silverton, built after the turn of the century, uses a cruciform plan.

206. The long, central first-floor hall of the Ouray County Courthouse is flanked by county offices.

207. This second-floor courtroom in the Teller County Courthouse, Cripple Creek, has beautiful hardwood wainscoting, a common wall treatment in public buildings.

Jails

Although some robberies and shootings occurred, lawmen in the mining communities spent most of their time pursuing drunks, dogs, and other nuisances. In addition, townspeople were often after the sheriff and his men to clean up the gambling holes and parlor houses. In early towns there were three types of punishment: public horsewhipping for minor crimes; temporary or permanent banishment from the town for more serious crimes; and hanging for murder, robbery, horse stealing, and other grave offenses.[1]

Several early jails were constructed of wood. Examples in Red Mountain and Animas Forks still remain. The town of Irwin had a four-cell wood jail of spiked together two-by-sixes. At least one outlaw is said to have destroyed himself in attempting to burn his way out of a wood jail.

For purposes of security, the use of stone in jail construction was soon widespread. The small, square, one-story jails of uncoursed stone usually have a watchman's area to the front and cells behind, as illustrated in the two-cell Georgetown jail (fig. 208). The back wall of the Silver Plume jail, in use from 1875 to 1915, was the rock cliff against which the building was constructed (fig. 209). Small stone jails can also be found in Central City (1860) and Telluride.

Larger, two-story brick jails appeared later, near the turn of the century. In Cripple Creek, the sheriff's office and jail were combined in a two-story brick structure with the offices on the first floor and the cells above (fig. 210). A decorative cornice of brickwork and round-arched Romanesque window openings give the structure an appropriate fortresslike appearance. This jail is still in operation today. Another two-story example can be found in Silverton (fig. 211). Built in 1903, it includes the sheriff's residence with private entrance, as well as an office, women's cell, and kitchen, on the first floor. An office, bath, and men's cells occupy the second floor. Of interest is the use of the Gilbert Iron Arched Ceiling, consisting of

208. This early, crude, stone jail in Georgetown contains a watchman's area and two cells.

209. This primitive stone jail in Silver Plume, used from 1875 to 1915, was built into the cliff that serves as its rear wall.

210. The two-story brick Cripple Creek jail and sheriff's office employs fortresslike Romanesque Revival detailing, a fitting style for a jail.

211. The Silverton jail, built in 1903, contains the sheriff's residence, one woman's cell, the kitchen, and an office on the first floor, with an office and men's cells on the second. The brick structure is now a museum.

corrugated, concave-arched, metal plates between I beams, covered with concrete to form the floor above (figs. 212, 213). Iron doors and stairways, barred windows, and fifteen-inch-thick brick walls combine with this rigid and durable ceiling construction to create an impregnable quality (figs. 214, 215).

City Halls

In most mining towns, the city hall included the local fire department. Small camps had simple log and frame buildings exemplified by the St. Elmo Fire Company and City Hall (fig. 216), a small, one-room, frame structure whose pitched roof is topped with a characteristic bell tower. In the more prosperous towns, city halls, like

212. The Gilbert Iron Arched Ceiling gives an impregnable quality to the Silverton jail.

213. A section of the Gilbert Iron Arched Ceiling shows its rigid construction.

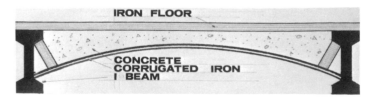

214. A second-floor men's cell in the Silverton jail.

215. An iron security door at the back of the Cripple Creek jail.

216. The simple wood frame fire company and city hall of the mining camp of St. Elmo is topped by a belfry for fire alarms.

215

214

216

courthouses, vary in style depending on the period during which they were constructed, although their interior plans are similar. These two-story buildings range in style from wood false fronts, seen in the Crested Butte City Hall and Fire Company (1883) and the Goldfield City Hall and Fire Station (1899) (figs. 217, 218), to elaborate brick Colonial Revival, as in the Victor City Hall (1900) (fig. 219).

The typical city hall has a large first-floor entrance leading to an open space for fire fighting equipment and to second-floor city offices. A bell tower for fire alarms sits atop the building or to the side. Many of the original city halls are still in operation today.

Firehouses

Fire was a constant danger in the mining communities. The wood frame structures that predominated were extremely vulnerable, and at one time or another most towns were ravaged by flames. As a result, firehouses were important in all towns. When a fire was spotted all the town bells were rung, train whistles sounded, and guns shot in the sky. Dynamiting of buildings to stop the spread of fire was

217. The city hall and fire company of Crested Butte was built in 1883. The wood frame Victorian structure, now a theater, includes first-floor fire equipment space and second-story town offices.

218. The wood frame Goldfield City Hall and Fire Station, built in 1899, features a characteristic bell tower for fire alarms and hose drying. A bracketed cornice crowns the otherwise unadorned face.

219. Colonial Revival detailing from the turn of the century dominates the facade of the brick city hall and fire station of Victor, shown here during a snowfall. The fire station and city hall share the first floor, with additional office space above. An elaborately detailed cornice and tower top the 1900 structure.

common. Quick rebuilding took place in prosperous towns. Brick buildings were under construction only five days after the Victor fire of 1899 as more than a thousand people helped rebuild the town. One day after the Victor fire, the post office had been reconstructed and mail was delivered, while saloons and restaurants were back in business in tents.

Not all firehouses were associated with city halls; some occupied their own buildings. Although some were simple, garagelike, one-story brick buildings like Hose

Company No. 2 in Idaho Springs (fig. 220) and Cripple Creek Fire Company No. 3, there were some flamboyant Victorian firehouses. Georgetown, whose four hose companies prevented its destruction, has several fine remaining examples of this firehouse style (figs. 221, 222). Usually two-story wood structures, they are similar to the city halls in plan with a large open space on the first floor for hose-cart storage and meeting rooms and offices on the second floor. Bell towers, used for fire lookouts and hose drying, are capped with elaborately decorated belfries.

Fire-fighting equipment included a small steam pump on wheels with a single hose (fig. 223). The companies took great pride in having a good hose-cart racing team. Cisterns holding water were strategically placed at main intersections for use in fire fighting. A later refinement was the addition of fire hydrants supplied by the city waterworks. The equipment of the Star Hook and Ladder Company of Georgetown differed from the usual hose company, as described in the following account:

> As opposed to a regular hose company, the Star Hook and Ladder boys pulled behind them the long truck with the ladders, hooks and leather water buckets on its side. They were an important refinement of the early fire fighting force. Their building was similar in design to the other hose houses, with equipment storage on the lower floor and a meeting hall upstairs.[2]

Georgetown has the best remaining examples of independent firehouses, but others can be found in many towns.

220. This simple, garagelike brick hose company is in Idaho Springs.

221. Plain, false-fronted Alpine Hose Company No. 2 in Georgetown, built in 1874, follows the usual firehouse plan of first-floor equipment storage area and second-floor meeting rooms. The bell tower, added in 1880, was used for hose drying and fire lookout.

222. The Star Hook and Ladder Company of Georgetown, built in the 1870s, features Italian detailing in the form of quoining at the corners, a bracket-supported balcony, and a decorative cupola.

223. Fire-fighting equipment usually included a hose cart of this type. Hose cart races between rival fire companies were popular.

Schools

In the early stages of the mining towns, children were taught in private homes or in the open air. When enough people arrived to organize a school district, an election would be called in order to raise bonds to build a permanent school building and hire teachers. The early log and clapboard-sided frame structures which resulted were simple one- and two-room rectangular affairs; some had a projecting entrance vestibule and a belfry atop the pitched roof (figs. 224–26). Many of these schools had

224. This early one-room frame schoolhouse in St. Elmo, built on a stone and log foundation, is topped by a crude belfry.

225. With its belfry-capped vestibule, this one-room schoolhouse in the South Park City Museum (Fairplay) is typical of its period. Simple Greek pediments top the window and door openings of the building, constructed in 1879.

226. The interior of the one-room schoolhouse at South Park City contains original period furnishings.

no blackboards and had to collect books from local families. Workloads were heavy; one teacher in Howardsville was expected to instruct a total of twenty-six classes each day, with all grades, from first through ninth, in one room at the same time. As the towns grew and the school populations increased, larger, more permanent schoolhouses were constructed, but poor, less prosperous towns continued using these one- and two-room structures. In Gold Hill, a two-room schoolhouse built in 1873 is still in service.

The larger, two-story schoolhouses followed the same general plan: classrooms on each floor flank a central hallway, which is reflected on the exterior as a projecting, often gable-topped element in the middle of the hip-roofed symmetrical form. Rooftop belfries are common additions. Although most schoolhouses of this type were constructed of brick, a fine wood example exists in Black Hawk (fig. 227), and one constructed by Cornish stonemasons in 1870 remains in Central City. Exterior detailing,

227. This two-story wood frame schoolhouse in Black Hawk uses a space arrangement typical of a larger school, with central hallway flanked by classrooms and an auditorium.

mainly Italianate influenced, takes the form of an occasional bracketed roof overhang, decorative window lintels, and towerlike belfries; Romanesque Revival, with its heavy, round-arched openings is also influential (figs. 228, 229). Many such structures still function today as local schoolhouses.

Churches

Traveling preachers were common. Father John L. Dyer, the famous itinerant "snowshoe" preacher, went to Buckskin Joe in 1861 to preach to the miners. He was over fifty years old at the time. Within two months he covered five hundred miles, collected forty-three dollars, and covered many of the early gold mining camps in Colorado. There were many of these traveling ministers, who served an important pastoral function until permanent churches could be established. To reach the smaller camps, they had to make long trips over rugged terrain, on horseback and in stagecoaches. The following notice appeared in the *Telluride Journal* in 1902: "Yesterday afternoon, Father O'Rourke, a Catholic priest, well known and very popular throughout the entire San Juan, and John McComb, a well known mining man, were drowned in the Animas River about 12 miles above Silverton."[3]

Like other early establishments, the first churches were located in tents and in simple log and canvas structures. In small towns, meetings were held practically anywhere, even in saloons and gambling houses. When the congregation grew, articles of incorporation were drawn up, a board of trustees was selected, a pastor was hired, and a church was built.

228. The brick Georgetown Public School features Italian detailing in the form of window and door lintels and a bracketed roof overhang. The elementary grades met on the first floor and the high school on the second. Built in 1874, the structure originally had three towers.

229. The more elaborate brick and stone Telluride High School, built in 1895, includes many classrooms on either side of a central corridor and displays exterior Romanesque detailing of round arches and rough masonry.

Many faiths were represented in the mining towns; Lutheran, Episcopal, Presbyterian, Catholic, Methodist, Baptist, Christian Scientist, and Congregational were among the most popular denominations. The church was the center of family social activities. The backbone of the churches were the various ladies aid societies, which organized picnics, lawn socials, Christmas parties, and the like.

The most common church design is not unlike that of the one-room schoolhouse, with simple rectangular plan and a central projecting entrance vestibule (fig. 230). Belfries, often capped by spires or finials, sit at the apex of the pitched roof or at the

230. St. Patrick's Church in Telluride uses simple Gothic detailing including lancet windows, a rose window over the vestibule, and a small belfry. It was built in 1896 for $4,800.

top of a tower above the vestibule (figs. 231, 232). This type of church is distinguished from the one-room schoolhouse chiefly by the liberal application of familiar Gothic detailing in the form of lancet windows; decorative bell towers and animated gables with pierced aprons; bargeboards; scalloped shingles; and often a centrally located rose window (figs. 233, 234). Interiors are characterized by straight wooden pews on either side of a wide center aisle, a simple altar, an occasional choir loft over the entrance, and a familiar wood-burning stove for heat (fig. 235).

As a parish grew more prosperous, its original church was enlarged or replaced, and a parsonage was often built for the pastor. In the larger, more elaborate brick and stone churches that followed with prosperity, the Gothic detailing became more elaborate and was joined by Italian, Queen Anne, and Romanesque influences. The bell tower became an even more important vertical element, often located to one side or the other rather than at the apex of the roof (figs. 236, 237). Although most churches of this type retained the general rectangular plan and pitched roof, a few Queen

231. The simple Sheldon Jackson Memorial Chapel in Fairplay, built in 1874, displays fine Gothic detailing. The board-and-batten-sided structure is capped by a beautiful belfry.

232. The wood frame Presbyterian Church in Lake City was erected in 1876. The bell tower, a dominant element, rises above the projecting vestibule.

233. Many Gothic churches are adorned with simple rose windows like this one on St. Patrick's Church, Telluride.

234. Some church entrances were elaborate, as this ornately carved Gothic example in Silver Plume illustrates.

235. The Sheldon Jackson Memorial Chapel in Fairplay contains a plain interior, with a central aisle bordered by wooden pews Most small churches followed this floor plan.

Anne–influenced structures introduced irregular arrangements and complex intersecting roof planes (fig. 238). The intricate use of stained glass was an important addition to window treatment (fig. 239). Although pews still flanked a central aisle, the interior space was sometimes given a traditionally European treatment, with vaulted ceilings and elaborate altars (fig. 240).

A few rare churches shed Gothic detailing altogether. St. Peter's Catholic Church

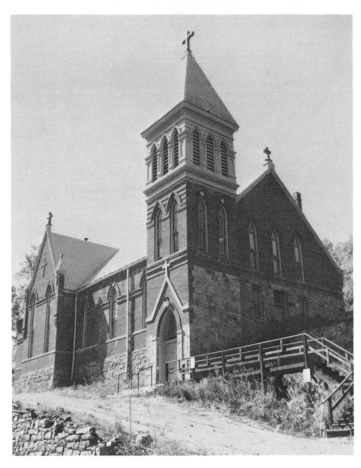

236. The stone and brick St. Mary's Church in Central City represents a later, more complex interpretation of the Gothic style.

237. The off-center bell tower of the Church of the Annunciation in Leadville is said to support the highest spire in the United States, beginning at 10,000 feet above sea level.

238. The Presbyterian Church of Leadville, constructed in 1890, combines the Queen Anne influence of complex roof planes with familiar Gothic detailing.

239. Stained glass windows were popular additions to later churches. This fine example is found in the Presbyterian Church in Leadville.

240. Interior church spaces often became elaborate, in some cases recalling European cathedrals. This is the interior of the Church of the Annunciation, Leadville.

135

(1897) in Cripple Creek is a pure Romanesque attempt, reminiscent of earlier European models. In sharp contrast to the Gothic majority, the Christian Scientist Church in Victor, which looks more like a Greek temple, exemplifies the Colonial and Georgian Revival influences felt near the turn of the century (fig. 241).

Many examples of Victorian church architecture can be found throughout the mining communities. Nearly all continue to operate today as they did in the nineteenth century.

Other Institutional Buildings

Some hospitals were built in the more prosperous towns to supplement doctors' offices. Diseases in mining communities included typhoid, pneumonia, diphtheria, scarlet fever, smallpox, Rocky Mountain spotted fever, and rheumatism. Industrial accidents were common, as explosions and falls often occurred at the mines. In addition, snow blindness, exposure, and frostbite were hazards for men who worked outdoors.

Examples of the two-story brick and stone hospitals, though no longer functioning as such, can be found in Telluride, Ouray, and Cripple Creek. The Telluride hospital, built in 1892, following no particular style, resembles a large schoolhouse from the exterior. Interiors usually provided wide corridors, wide staircases, and lifts for the conveyance of the sick from floor to floor; interior spaces included entrance and waiting room, kitchen, offices, patient wards, and crude operating facilities.

Some of the larger towns had public libraries and reading rooms. In 1880, Central

241. The Christian Scientist Church in Victor, erected in the early 1900s, breaks from the Gothic tradition with a Colonial Revival interpretation. The church is deserted today.

City had a well-selected library of 2,000 volumes. The public libraries, however, were few and far between; the circulating library was more common:

> Operating usually from a local store, or perhaps a rented room, it was open to those who were willing to pay the monthly or yearly dues. The number of acquisitions remained small, probably in the low hundreds, and the variety depended on the group ordering the books. . . .[4]

Few examples of library buildings, if any, remain.

The National Guard and military companies, which put down both Indian and labor threats, were headquartered in armories. Because of their large, open interior spaces, the two-story brick structures, like the remaining armory halls in Lake City and Central City, often served a variety of functions. Armory Hall in Central City served as both a theater and a firehouse at different times.

7

Industrial Architecture

Mining

The mining towns we have been discussing would never have existed in the first place were it not for the discovery and mining of precious metals at or near their point of evolution. All activities in the mining communities were secondary to mining itself. Miners were generally intelligent, kindhearted, sociable men. Often roughly dressed in blue jeans or overalls, hobnailed boots, rubber boots for working in waterlogged mines, broad-brimmed hats, undershirts, and overshirts, the miners worked long, hard hours. Although they lived in crude log and frame cabins, they ate the finest food available and drank profusely, as indicated by their high alcoholism rate. Lonely hearts clubs and mail-order brides were common, as most early miners were single and very few unmarried females lived in the camps. Many foreigners worked the mines, among them Cornishmen, Welshmen, Italians, Austrians, Irishmen, and Chinese. As a contemporary put it, "The reports of prizes drawn by the few and of opportunities afforded the many were the magnetic influences that attracted the less fortunate mortals from abroad."[1]

Nearly every business and professional man in the towns was involved in backing miners or prospectors. A backer usually furnished a grubstake of supplies or wages to men who would sink a shaft. In this way a number of men were furnished employment and many a paying mine resulted.

Most rich lodes were discovered entirely by accident, as illustrated by the following accounts:

> . . . Up at the top of Jonny Hill is the mine which made John Campion a multimillionaire. Like many another mine it was found by chance, when an

Englishman with pick and shovel stopped to ask a geologist where to dig and the geologist, busy and disinterested, answered, "Underneath that tree." The Englishman dug and struck the Little Jonny which became one of the richest mines in Leadville.[2]

The Mackey mine at Apex was similarly found by accident:

> The mine was originally owned by Dick Mackey. It was taken over by a fellow named Mountz and his partners. They had hardly begun work on the mine when the partners ran off with $30,000, leaving Mountz with a grand total of $400 in working capital.
>
> Mountz did all he could, working carefully and frugally. He drove in a tunnel. No good, the money ran out. In disgust Mountz planted dynamite to blow up the whole mess. The blast uncovered a rich lode. Mountz ordered a bundle of ore sacks from Denver on credit. He ordered two four-horse teams and wagons from Central City on credit. He was in business. The first ore assayed at $1,800 a ton. Mountz paid up his bills and didn't need any credit after that.[3]

In still another account, silver was found by accident by two old prospectors who had worked constantly for nearly two years and found nothing. By the second summer they were completely disgruntled. One day, sitting on a slab of rock, one of them said: "Ain't anything in this country. Worked it for two years without a strike." As he spoke he struck the rock with his hammer. "Think I'll pack up and pull out," he continued. With a second blow a chunk broke off the rock and dropped—but not to the ground, for it was suspended by wires from the large rock mass. Leaping to their feet to investigate this phenomenon, the men discovered that wire silver was holding the severed fragment securely to the rocky ledge. The two canceled all plans to leave the region that instant, staked off a claim, and had their ore assayed. It was 80 percent solid silver. Thus began the Fairview mine, which produced steadily until 1893.[4]

Miners' laws varied from district to district. Early laws concerning mining claims in Gilpin County specified that no miner could hold a claim along more than one creek or on more than one mountain and that placer claims could be no more than one hundred feet square and lode claims no more than one hundred feet long and fifty feet wide. The average cost of securing a claim or patent in 1880 was between one hundred twenty-five and one hundred sixty dollars. In the same year, not less than a hundred thousand claims of various sorts had been filed, of which only a few thousand were actually being worked at the time. In addition to claim jumping, mining laws in Fulford, near Glenwood Springs, provided a legal way to get another's claim:

> The mining laws stated any claim, not proved up on by midnight of the fiscal year, was open for relocation. Anyone intrepid enough to get there and drive new stakes could own the property. Miners could eye a good

claim enviously and keep tabs to see if the owner was doing the required amount of work. If he was not, woe to him! A new claimant would be driving stakes on his mine while he toasted in the New Year at some saloon.[5]

Colorado winters were long and cold; most mining was done in the summer. In winter most miners went to warmer places such as Denver or back to their homes in the East or elsewhere, returning in the spring for another digging season.

MINING METHODS AND RELATED STRUCTURES

In placer mining, the first method used by the early prospectors, gold is removed from alluvial deposits of sand, gravel, and dirt. The gold, which is located throughout the gravel, or pay dirt, lodges in considerable quantities at the bottom of streams while the lighter elements are carried downstream by the current. In placer mining the gold is washed from the pay dirt and secured in pans, flumes, and sluice boxes; quicksilver (mercury) was often used to retain it in swift running water, due to its unique affinity to the precious metal. In operations of great magnitude, large sums of money were often expended in bringing an adequate water supply to the placer diggings. When no water was nearby, miles of ditches and flumes were often built. Powerful hydraulics were commonly used like giant fire hoses to wash against the hillsides and expose the deposits; at a later date, dredges were also used.

Early prospectors searched the country for mineralized areas, identifiable by the presence of "quartz" everywhere. The term *quartz* was applied to gold, silver, and other ores in their original state, varying in value from nothing at all to thousands of dollars per ton. Samples of the mineralized rock were delivered to assay offices, where they were analyzed for presence and quantity of metallic elements. The small assay offices were usually furnished with a desk, cupboards, shelves of reference books and mineral specimens, prospecting equipment, an assay furnace, assaying glassware and crates of crucibles, and balances. The office was usually covered with a layer of rock dust (figs. 242, 243).

As lodes were discovered, shafts were sunk vertically and tunnels were excavated horizontally. Shaft operations were impracticable in precipitous locations, so numerous tunnels were sunk in these areas. No hoist is required in a tunnel mine, and only an adit, or entrance, is visible, with a dump of waste rock usually displayed nearby (fig. 244). Both the waste rock, or gangue, and the valuable ore were removed from this type of mine by methods including foot-powered ore carts that ran on tracks and horse- or mule-drawn ore wagons. Colorful mule skinners drove the wagons wearing blue jeans with cuffs turned up one inch for each mule in the team; there were usually six or eight mules in a team.

The shaft mine, in contrast, was mounted initially by a hand-powered windlass, later replaced by a gallows, or headframe, "a heavily braced right triangle, between

242. This typical early log assay office, from the nearby North London mine, is now located in the South Park City Museum (Fairplay). Here a miner could find out the value or grade of his ore.

243. The gravel-floored interior of the North London mine assay office contains shelves filled with ore samples, scales, and retorts.

whose vertical legs are the shaft and shaft collar, the latter topped by a substantial platform equipped with tracks or a sheet iron floor"[6] (figs. 245, 246). Shaft openings varied in size. One such opening, at the main shaft of the Caribou mine, was 5 feet by 14 feet. Its double-hoisting bucketway reached a depth of 810 feet (fig. 247).

Buckets of ore were initially drawn from the shaft, which met different levels of intersecting horizontal tunnels, through the gallow frame by way of horse power. At the London mine at Mosquito Pass, a windmill was built to provide power. Water, however, was the major source of power before electricity. The hoist and pumps were run by steam produced by burning wood. Electric generating power plants were not

244. A mine entrance or adit near Silver Plume. The rails leading from the mouth were used to transport carts of ore.

245. A primitive horse-drawn or hand-pulled gallow frame in the South Park City Museum (Fairplay). Buckets carrying ore and miners ascended and descended the shaft between the legs of this heavy-timbered structure.

246. The Queen mine in Elkton is the site of this heavy-timbered gallow frame with attached ore storage bin, shown here amid falling snow.

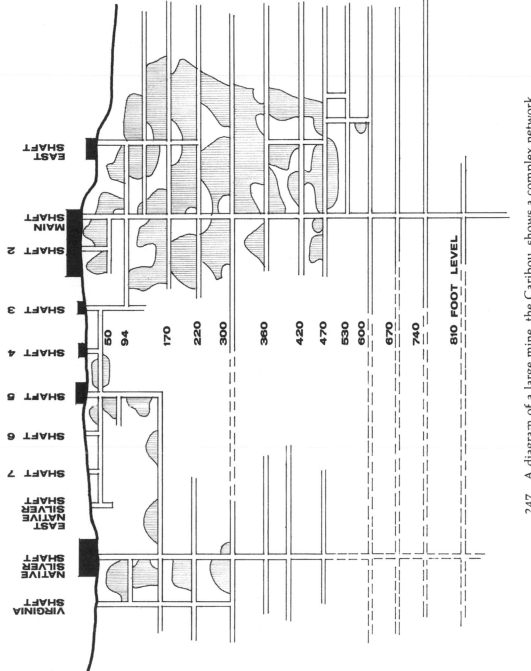

247. A diagram of a large mine, the Caribou, shows a complex network of intersecting shafts and tunnels.

set up until the 1890s. The Revenue mine in Sneffels was the first mine to use electric power.

In addition to ore chutes, shaft houses often accompanied the headframe (figs. 248, 249). Usually spacious, the shaft room included a space for storing timbers for the mine, a machine room with the hoisting equipment, and a blacksmith room. The engine and hoisting machinery were sometimes located underground, depending upon the positions of shafts and tunnels in the mine.

Interior timbering was a method used to prevent cave-ins, as indicated by the following description:

> As the ore is taken out, the ground above is kept from caving in by "square sets" composed of massive timbers two feet more or less in diameter. The upright posts are from seven to ten feet high, and these are capped by similar timbers from four to five feet wide. Thus one set is built above another until the top of the cavity once containing the ore is reached.[7]

Most mines were threatened by water seepage. The problem became worse as lower levels were reached, and pumps were installed to drain the mines. Tunnels were often dug to drain the lower levels of permanently flooded mines. The mines that could not afford such procedures were forced to close down.

The interior of the Bobtail mine at Black Hawk is described as having had huge engines and boilers for running the pumps and hoists. The shaft was 8 feet by 16 feet and ran 400 feet below the tunnel level. It was divided into four parts—one for sinking, one for the pump and ladder way, and two for the cageways, descending and ascending, bringing up men, supplies, and ore. The cars, each carrying two tons of ore, were run on the iron tracks of the various levels of the mine to the shaft and then loaded on the cageways for the trip to the top. Upon leaving the tunnel or shaft, the waste rock was dumped and the ore carts were rolled on tracks to ore storage bins where their contents were deposited. The heavy-timbered ore bins were provided with chutes to allow for the easy loading of the wagons which would transport the ore to the nearest mill (figs. 250, 251). When mills were close at hand, ore was often transported directly to them from the mine.

The headworks of a mining operation usually included offices, living quarters if no town was adjacent, ore bins, shops, change rooms, and storage yards for timbers and machinery. Some company towns existed. One such town, St. Johns, included a two-and-one-half-story boardinghouse, company store, assay office, guesthouse, mess hall, foreman's house, superintendent's home, and miners' houses. Company bunkhouses were usually large barracklike structures with open bays where miners slept in double- or triple-deck bunks. Some were partitioned off into rooms. Usually the company furnished the mattresses and the miners supplied their own sheets and pillows. A miners' boardinghouse at Camp Bird mine near Ouray housed 400 men and offered electric lights, steam heat, modern sewage, marble-top lavatories, and reading rooms. In order to avoid avalanche problems, this structure was built into the hill and the roof pitched in such a manner that the slides could run over the building

248. A headframe and ore chutes of wood and corrugated metal near Idaho Springs.

249. This snowy scene in Goldfield features a more elaborate headworks with gallow frame and connecting shaft house.

without knocking it down. At times ten to eighteen feet of snow stood on the roof and the building could be entered only through a tunnel in the snow.

Ore Transportation

Before the arrival of the railroad, freight wagons were used to haul ore to the nearest mill, smelter, or completed railhead. Sometimes pulled by as many as eight mules, the wagons, which often traveled in trains, looked like snakes slithering around the mountains. The cost of hauling a wagonload of ore across the pass from Tin Cup to St. Elmo was $3.50. When the snow got too deep, sleds, in place of wagons, were often used to transport the ore to the railroads.

Aerial tramways were commonly used to transport ore from high mountainous mines to mills and railroads or from higher remote mines to lower ones, where the ore was in turn hauled away by wagons or sleds. Early tramways operated on the principle of gravity whereby the full buckets going down forced the empty ones back up. Electric tramways followed; these could carry up to forty ore buckets placed at intervals of 600 feet on one cable and reach speeds of 6 feet per second. Heavy-timbered terminals at both ends usually included an ore house, an apparatus

250. A heavy-timbered ore storage bin in Virginia Canyon near Idaho Springs. The chutes at the bottom fed ore to wagons for transportation to the mill.

251. This massive ore house is at the Commodore mine near Creede. Ore dumped from carts at the top is removed to wagons through ore chutes at the bottom.

for operating the tram, and storage quarters. The spacing of the towers depended on the terrain to be crossed (fig. 252). Descending cars carried the ore, while ascending buckets carried blasting powder, coal, timbers, and miners. The aerial trams often covered great distances, like the two-mile tram that brought the ore from the Camp Bird mine to the mill.

Mills, Smelters, and Associated Buildings

Early ore-crushing methods included the use of the Spanish arrastra, a circular floor over which horses dragged stones to pulverize the ore. This primitive method was quickly replaced by large stamp and quartz mills which implemented a relatively complex wet crushing process. The mill proper consisted of a solid framework, crushers, and heavy iron stamps and attachments, propelled by steam or water power by means of a horizontal shaft and connections. Operations began when the ore, carried in the narrow, high-sided wagons, by carts on rails, or by aerial trams, was delivered to the mill's ore platform or storage bins. Often a crusher man, after having reduced the ore to fist size with a sledgehammer, would direct it down a chute to a

252. A heavy wood tram tower leading to the Kentucky Belle mine near Creede aided in ore transportation.

crusher, where it was further reduced in size. From the crusher the ore usually went to a stamp mill, where heavy stamps, dropping on it from twenty-seven to thirty-five times per minute from heights of twelve to eighteen inches, further pulverized the ore (fig. 253). While the ore was shoveled onto the inclined tables or troughs as fast as it was crushed by the stamps, a continuous stream of water flowed in the same direction. Some mills had only a single battery of stamps; others had as many as sixty.

The crushed ore would then slide onto copper-plated tables, where mercury was often added, as both copper and mercury have an affinity for gold and silver. This operation kept most of the gold on the tables while waste was carried onward by the water to the nearest stream or tank. Occasionally the stamps were stopped and the table cleaned. The gold and quicksilver mixture was carried to the retort room where it was skimmed, cleaned, and pressed in a cloth to get rid of as much mercury as possible. The remainder was retorted, and the crude bullion was sold at banks or shipped.

In the process of retorting, the amalgam of gold and mercury is placed in clay-lined iron retorts. When heated, the mercury passes through a pipe as vapor and

253. Diagram of a typical ten-stamp mill. Ore is pulverized under the pounding weights.

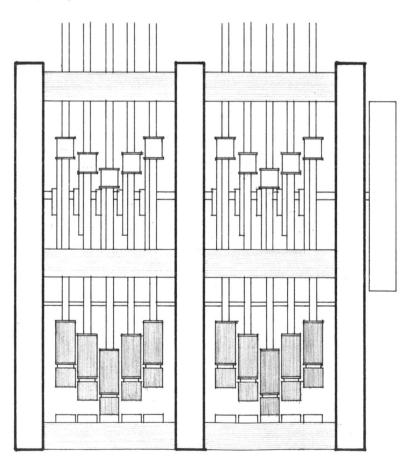

condenses again into mercury in the bucket to which it has passed. The gold remains pure in the retort. Gold was cast in the shape of a brick and stamped with its weight and the name of the company; it was then ready for market. Although large quantities of gold and silver were lost by this type of milling process, it was one of the cheapest methods and therefore suitable for low-grade ores. The cost of this treatment in 1880 was from two to three dollars per ton of ore.

Although over a hundred small quartz mills or stamp mills of five, ten, or fifteen stamps were located in Gilpin County in the earlier years, only a few were in use at any one time. By 1880 there were twenty mills and eight hundred stamps at work.

Many other processes followed the same basic method, as pulverization of the ore by stamps, crushers, and rolls was necessary before the silver and gold could be extracted. Roasting the crushed ore in revolving cylinders, a more expensive process, retained more of the precious metals. In a more modern recovery process used in Victor, the crushed ore was placed in large vats, where it was treated with a solution of sodium or calcium cyanide which dissolved the gold.

The functional form of the milling structures was a direct result of the mountainous terrain, the snowy climate, and the natural gravity-related sequence of interior operations in the mills. The buildings slope and step down rugged hillsides, reflecting the step-by-step downhill process of ore crushing (figs. 254, 255). The large buildings were generally constructed of heavy timbers and massive wood trusses, although the Gold Prince mill at Animas Forks used steel members. Corrugated metal roofs and siding were common. Windows either opened above the roof of the successive lower plane, clerestory fashion, or stepped down the sides from level to level.

Concrete was occasionally used for foundations or walls in commercial, residential, and institutional architecture, but it was a common building material in the mining and milling structures. Although earlier mining-related buildings had stone foundations, many that followed used concrete, an enduring substance that provided reliable support for heavy loads. Cribbing and shoring were often used to build up foundations on sloping sites (fig. 256).

Concentrating mills, functioning on the same general gravity-flow principle as other mills, were often used to concentrate the ore before shipment to smelters. In order to avoid the extra cost of shipping worthless material, the ore was crushed and passed through a series of sizing screens. Continuous washing would allow the heavier portions, containing the valuable metals, to work their way to the bottom while the lighter, useless material was carried away by the water. The resulting concentrate was collected and shipped to the smelter. One such mill, the Gold King, was 460 feet long, had a floor space of about 25,000 square feet, employed forty men, and cost $350,000. The mill used first twenty, later forty, and then eighty stamps; its daily production was sixty tons of concentrate.

It was difficult to extract the gold and silver from ores carrying a high lead content without a blast smelting furnace. Usually the smelter or reduction works were a long way from the mines, so it was expensive to carry the ore. Before the arrival of the railroad, many small smelters were scattered throughout the towns. With the

254. Reflecting its gravity-related function, this mill near Silverton slopes down the hill.

255. A spectacular example of mill architecture, the Argo mill in Idaho Springs also reflects the downhill processes of ore refinement.

2.56. Cribbing was often used to support mining structures on sloping sites. This example is in Idaho Springs.

advent of rail transportation, shipments to larger, centrally located smelters could be made. In the remote areas, the rich ores were sent on mule or burro trains over the passes to the nearest railhead to go to the smelters.

These sheet-iron furnaces were usually circular, taller than their diameter. They were built so that ore, coke, charcoal, and slag or iron could be fed from an upper floor into the body of the furnace, while the melted lead, silver, and slag would make their way out from separate outlets at the base of the furnace in the story below. The hot liquids were poured into molds and cooled into bars. Reverberatory brick furnaces were also common. They were often forty to sixty feet long and divided into separate compartments or hearths.

The first smelting works in Colorado was built in Black Hawk in 1868. Before that time all ores to be smelted were shipped out of the state, a costly process. Because smelting works were often located in flat valley sites, their exterior appearance differed from that of the slope-clinging mills. One large, rectangular valley smelter at Golden was described as follows:

> The plant consisted of a substantially erected main building built of corrugated iron, both roof and sides. Two six-ton calcining furnaces, one fifteen-ton reverbatory furnace, two twenty-two ton water jacket blast furnaces, two cupel furnaces, a complete set of tanks for the separation of copper from copper matte, a thirty-five-horse-power engine, a forty-five-horse-power boiler, two Blake crushers and rolls for crushing and all necessary equipment for sampling. Attached to the office there was also a complete laboratory for assaying and analysis. Twenty tons of ore were handled daily.[8]

One plant, with a large smelter yard where the ore trains were loaded and unloaded, had a main building 450 feet long and 120 feet wide. Inside were scales for weighing cars, steam engines for operating crushing and sampling machinery, and ten calciners, each of which could roast 9,600 pounds of ore in twenty-four hours. Adjoining the main building were thirty roasting kilns and a smokestack 100 feet high that carried off fumes from both the kilns and the calciners. All the buildings were constructed of cut stone and roofed with corrugated iron. Leadville had many smelters due to the large quantities of lead in the vicinity. Idaho Springs and Durango were also major smelting centers.

Although they are disappearing rapidly, many fine examples of the mining architecture of earlier times can be found. The skeletons of headframes, shaft houses, ore bins, and mills are scattered throughout the mountains as a reminder of more prosperous times. Smelter remains are rare; occasional solitary smokestacks flag their earlier locations.

Other Industrial Structures

Other than mining, industrial activities were minimal, as almost everything was shipped in from the East. Few remains of these other industries are evident today.

Foundries, which made mining equipment, including stamps and machinery, were common. The remains of the oldest foundry in Colorado can be found in Central City. In addition, Durango, Denver, Colorado Springs, and Leadville had ironworks that produced cast-iron products, including some metal storefronts. Another small industry was the production of sheet-iron products and boilers. One such factory, which was also a machine shop, remains in Leadville.

Sawmills, powered by both waterwheels and steam, appeared in great numbers, producing the lumber for town construction. In addition, some mines had complete sawmill and lumber-dressing plants right on the site to provide wood for surface buildings and for the interior bracings of the mine. In 1880, Leadville, with a population of fifteen thousand, had fifteen sawmills operating. Remains are rare; fire destroyed many of the mills, and others have simply rotted away.

Initially bricks were shipped in from the East, but when demand became great enough, bricks, available in many colors, began to be produced locally. Golden and Denver were the primary sources of bricks for the mining communities.

The brewing of beer was one of the more important industries in many places. Beer was the most popular alcoholic beverage, and as it did not travel well, many a town had its own brewery. Fine stone examples can be found in Telluride and South Park City in Fairplay (fig. 257).

With the advent of electricity, gas factories were replaced by electric power plants. Many of the power plants were hastily thrown up: "The idea of establishing an electric plant in Creede was conceived at noon on February 1, 1892. Five days later the lights flickered on all over town!"[9] None of the old gasworks and few of the electric plants remain. A fine stone substation, representing the Pikes Peak Power Company, still stands in Victor (fig. 258).

257. Sumner's Brewery in the South Park City Museum (Fairplay) was constructed in 1873. South Park Lager Beer was produced in the stone building.

258. Romanesque detailing is blurred by snow in this view of the brick and stone Pikes Peak Power Company substation in Victor.

153

Epilogue

Many communities that died before the turn of the century, as mining activities decreased, have stood deserted and crumbling ever since. Others have staggered along, semiabandoned. Even in the few towns that have remained active and reasonably prosperous, however, few new buildings have been constructed during the seventy-odd years since major mining activity ceased. Furthermore, those original buildings that still stand are usually in bad condition through neglect or vandalism; many have collapsed, burned, or been torn down (fig. 259).

259. Fire continues to change and destroy towns. This fire in Durango occurred in August 1974.

Several towns, however, realizing the value of their heritage, are making serious attempts to maintain the original Victorian flavor. Local historical societies and other concerned citizens' groups have been instrumental in preservation through restoration and the implementation of strict zoning ordinances to control ski and land developments.

While some towns are doing their best to protect the original atmosphere, the abandoned communities and mining structures have been sadly neglected. Their deserted shells continue to deteriorate and invite vandalism. It would be desirable for the state to provide aid in preserving some of this heritage. The restoration of such mining structures and abandoned communities could lead to the creation of living museums with period activities, furnishings, and costumes, comparable to the restorations at Williamsburg, Virginia and Cades Cove in Great Smoky Mountains National Park.

Apart from a few efforts toward restoration, the atmosphere of nineteenth-century mining days is gone forever. I hope this book has given readers some understanding of that bygone era.

*   *   *

The last three decades of the nineteenth century in Colorado west of the Ramparts, the men who built the railroads, the mines, and the metals they exploited, the cities they built and abandoned, the tumults and the fanfares attendant upon vast and sudden riches, the pattern and color and pageantry of a human comedy, paralleled elsewhere but never quite duplicated on earth, are all now a part of the record and the legend.

—Lucius Beebe

Glossary

adit   A mine tunnel entrance.

architrave   The lowermost section of a classical entablature, consisting of architrave, frieze, and cornice, resting on the capitals of columns; also, more loosely, the molded frame surrounding a door or window.

archivolt   Arched detailing over openings, commonly found over Romanesque arched windows.

arrastra   A primitive ore-reducing machine consisting of a hard circular platform upon which the ore is deposited and crushed by means of a revolving sweep to which huge flat stones are attached.

balloon frame   House frame built up from small-dimensioned lumber, principally two-by-fours, nailed together.

balustrade   A row of turned or rectangular posts topped by a rail.

bargeboard   A board covering the end rafters of a gable. Also called a vergeboard. These wooden members are usually treated decoratively.

board-and-batten   Vertical plank siding with joints covered by narrow wood strips.

bonanza   A Spanish term signifying good luck or prosperity; also a large, rich ore body.

braced framing   A method of construction utilizing wood braces in support of wood framing.

bracket   A symbolic cantilever, usually of fanciful form, used under a cornice.

calciner   A furnace used for smelting ores.

chinking   Filling the spaces between the logs on a log cabin.

clapboard   Board siding laid horizontally and overlapping, butted vertically.

composition   A material composed of various ingredients, often taking the place of a more expensive or uncompounded substance and often used for decorative detailing on Victorian structures.

corner board   A vertical board at the end of a wall that has been covered with wooden siding, used to give the wall a neat edge. Also called pilaster board.

cornice   A decoratively treated horizontal molding at the edge of a roof.

cresting   An ornamental finish along the top of a roof; usually decorated and sometimes perforated.

cribbing   Heavy-timbered cratelike construction used to support structures on sloping sites.

cross gable   A gable set parallel to the roof ridge.

cruciform   Arranged in the shape of a cross.

dentil   A small, rectangular block forming one of a series applied as ornamentation below a cornice.

dormer   A window placed vertically in a sloping roof and with a roof of its own.

dripstone   A projecting molding to throw off the rain, on the face of a wall, above an arch, doorway, or window.

entablature   The upper part of an order, in classical architecture, consisting of architrave, frieze, and cornice.

finial   A Gothic ornament placed at the apex of a roof.

flume   Boxing or piping for conveying water.

gable   The triangular upper portion of a wall at the end of a pitched roof.

gangue   The waste rock of the ore.

gingerbread   Decorative woodwork applied to Victorian houses.

grubstake   To provide a miner with food and supplies in exchange for a portion of the findings of his prospecting.

hip roof   A roof with sloping ends and sides.

lancet window   A slender, pointed-arched window.

lintel   A horizontal beam or stone bridging an opening.

lode   A fissure filled with ore-bearing matter.

oriel window   An angular or curved projection of a building front filled by windows, identical to a bay window but found at upper floors only.

overdoor light   A glazed area above a doorway, often decoratively treated.

pay dirt   Dirt rich in precious minerals.

pediment   A triangular gable often used as an ornamental member over a doorway or window.

pierced apron   A perforated panel below a windowsill or at the apex of a gable space, sometimes shaped and decorated.

placer mining   The mining of gold-bearing alluvial deposits of dirt or gravel from streams.

plush   A fabric with a pile longer and softer than that of velvet; a popular Victorian furniture covering.

quoining   Heavy blocks, generally of stone or of wood cut to imitate stone, used at the corner of a building to reinforce masonry walls, or in wood or brick as a decorative feature.

reduction   The extraction of metals from ore.

saltbox   A one-and-one-half- or two-story colonial house with a long rear roof line.

segmental head   An arch which is a segment of a circle drawn from a center below the level at which the arch springs from its supports. Used in Italianate Victorian buildings over door and window openings.

sidelight   A narrow window area beside an outside door, common in Greek Revival.

sluice box   A trough through which gold-bearing gravel is washed.

string course   A continuous horizontal band, either plain or molded, projecting from the surface of a building at an upper floor level.

swag   An ornament in the form of a garland of flowers, a string of fruit, or a piece of drapery suspended between two points so as to sag gently in the middle.

tracery   The ornamental intersecting work in the upper part of a window, screen, or panel.

wainscot   Wood paneling applied to an interior wall.

widow's walk   A balustraded lookout on residential rooftops.

Appendix: List of Towns

The towns visited in preparing this study were among the most typical Colorado mining communities of the nineteenth century. Communities that were difficult to reach, those in deteriorated condition or complete ruin, and those of little importance or interest were eliminated unless unusual features or outstanding original buildings were present, or unless the community was near a major town. See figure 1 for locations of towns.

The following list gives a brief sketch of each town visited:

1. Location by county
2. Location by highway
3. Altitude
4. Approximate date of founding
5. Population at significant intervals (according to U.S. census)
6. Architectural points of interest, if any

ALMA

1. Park County
2. State Road 9
3. 10,300 ft.
4. Founded: Late 1870s
5. Population: 1880—446; 1890—367; 1900—297; 1970—73
6. Architectural points of interest: Almost destroyed by fire in 1937, the town has been rebuilt.

ASPEN

1. Pitkin County
2. State Road 82
3. 7,850 ft.
4. Founded: Early 1880s
5. Population: 1890—5,108; 1900—3,305; 1970—2,404
6. Architectural points of interest: Hotel Jerome; Aspen Opera House; many fine Victorian homes

BLACK HAWK

1. Gilpin County
2. Junction of State Roads 279 and 119
3. 8,032 ft.
4. Founded: Late 1850s
5. Population: 1870—1,068; 1880—1,540; 1890—1,067; 1900—1,200; 1960—171
6. Architectural points of interest: Lace House; main street commercial structures

BOULDER

1. Boulder County
2. U.S. 36
3. 5,530 ft.
4. Founded: Late 1850s
5. Population: 1870—343; 1880—3,069; 1890—3,330; 1900—6,150; 1970—66,870
6. Architectural points of interest: Main street commercial buildings; fine Victorian houses

BRECKENRIDGE

1. Summit County
2. State Road 9
3. 9,579 ft.
4. Founded: Early 1860s
5. Population: 1880—1,657; 1900—976; 1970—548
6. Architectural points of interest: Some fine log houses and Victorian homes; churches

CENTRAL CITY

1. Gilpin County
2. State Road 279
3. 8,560 ft.
4. Founded: Late 1850s
5. Population: 1860—598; 1870—2,360; 1890—2,480; 1900—3,114; 1970—228
6. Architectural points of interest: Entire town offers fine examples of residential, commercial, and institutional buildings including Gilpin County Courthouse, Central City Opera House, the Teller House, and main street commercial structures.

CREEDE

1. Mineral County
2. State Road 149
3. 8,854 ft.
4. Founded: Early 1890s
5. Population: 1900—938; 1970—653
6. Architectural points of interest: Train station; mining and milling structures

CRESTED BUTTE

1. Gunnison County
2. State Road 135
3. 9,000 ft.
4. Founded: Early 1880s
5. Population: 1890—857; 1900—988; 1970—372
6. Architectural points of interest: City Hall; churches; main street commercial buildings

CRIPPLE CREEK

1. Teller County
2. State Road 67
3. 9,375 ft.
4. Founded: Early 1890s
5. Population: 1900—10,147; 1970—425

6. Architectural points of interest: Entire town offers fine examples of residential, commercial, institutional, and industrial buildings including Teller County Courthouse, jail, Homestead Parlor House, railroad station, main street commercial buildings, and nearby mining structures.

DUMONT

1. Clear Creek County
2. Interstate 70
3. 7,955 ft.
4. Founded: Early 1860s
5. Population: 1890—139; 1900—200
6. Architectural points of interest: Mill City House

DURANGO

1. La Plata County
2. U.S. 550 and U.S. 160
3. 6,505 ft.
4. Founded: Early 1880s
5. Population: 1890—2,726; 1900—3,317; 1970—10,333
6. Architectural points of interest: Main street commercial structures; railroad station; Strater Hotel; many fine Victorian homes.

ELKTON

1. Teller County
2. State Road 67
3. Altitude not available
4. Founded: Mid 1890s
5. Population not available
6. Architectural points of interest: Mining structures

EMPIRE

1. Clear Creek County
2. State Road 40 and Interstate 70
3. 8,603 ft.
4. Founded: Mid 1860s
5. Population: 1890—134; 1900—276; 1970—249

FAIRPLAY

1. Park County
2. State Road 9
3. 9,964 ft.
4. Founded: Late 1850s
5. Population: 1890—301; 1900—319; 1970—419
6. Architectural points of interest: Park County Courthouse; Sheldon Jackson Memorial Chapel; South Park City Museum

FRISCO

1. Summit County

2. U.S. 6 and State Road 9
3. Altitude not available
4. Founded: Early 1880s
5. Population: 1970—471

GEORGETOWN

1. Clear Creek County
2. Interstate 70
3. 8,640 ft.
4. Founded: Early 1860s
5. Population: 1870—802; 1880—3,294; 1890—1,927; 1900—1,418; 1970—542
6. Architectural points of interest: Entire town offers fine examples of residential, commercial, and institutional buildings including Hotel de Paris, Hamill house, Maxwell house, firehouses, Victorian houses, and main street commercial structures.

GILLETT

1. Teller County
2. State Road 67
3. 9,938 ft.
4. Founded: Early 1890s
5. Population: 1900—524

GOLDFIELD

1. Teller County
2. State Road 67
3. Altitude not available
4. Founded: Mid 1890s
5. 1900—2,191
6. Architectural points of interest: City Hall and Fire Company; mining and milling structures

GOLD HILL

1. Boulder County
2. Four Mile Canyon Road
3. 8,500 ft.
4. Founded: Late 1850s
5. Population: 1890—425; 1900—407
6. Architectural points of interest: Miners' hotel; schoolhouse

IDAHO SPRINGS

1. Clear Creek County
2. Interstate 70
3. 7,500 ft.
4. Founded: Late 1850s
5. Population: 1860—255; 1870—229; 1880—733; 1890—1,338; 1900—2,502; 1970—2,003
6. Architectural points of interest: Fine Victorian houses; Argo mill and other nearby mining and milling structures

IRONTON

1. Ouray County
2. U.S. 550
3. 9,750 ft.
4. Founded: Early 1880s
5. Population: 1900—71; 1960—1
6. Architectural points of interest: Some log and early frame houses and barns

LAKE CITY

1. Hinsdale County
2. State Road 149
3. 8,500 ft.
4. Founded: Mid 1870s
5. Population: 1890—607; 1900—700; 1970—91
6. Architectural points of interest: Hinsdale County Courthouse; Victorian homes and churches

LAWSON

1. Clear Creek County
2. Interstate 70
3. Altitude not available
4. Founded: Mid 1870s
5. Population: 1900—285

LEADVILLE

1. Lake County
2. U.S. 24
3. 10,152 ft.
4. Founded: Late 1870s
5. Population: 1880—14,820; 1890—10,384; 1900—12,455; 1970—4,314
6. Architectural points of interest: Entire town offers fine examples of residential, commercial, institutional, and industrial buildings including Tabor Opera House; Tabor Grande Hotel; Tabor house, Healy house, and other Victorian houses; nearby mining and milling structures.

MATTERHORN

1. San Miguel County
2. State Road 145
3. Altitude not available
4. Founding date unknown
5. Population not available
6. Architectural points of interest: Log cabins; mining and milling remains.

MAYSVILLE

1. Chaffee County
2. U.S. 50
3. Altitude not available

4. Founded: Late 1870s
5. Population: 1900—86
6. Architectural points of interest: Schoolhouse

NEDERLAND

1. Boulder County
2. State Roads 72 and 119
3. 8,200 ft.
4. Founded: Early 1870s
5. Population: 1890—111; 1900—182; 1970—492

OPHIR AND OLD OPHIR

1. San Miguel County
2. State Road 145
3. 9,800 ft.
4. Founded: Mid 1870s
5. Population: 1880—130; 1890—113; 1900—127; 1970—6

OURAY

1. Ouray County
2. U.S. 550
3. 7,800 ft.
4. Founded: Mid 1870s
5. Population: 1880—864; 1890—2,534; 1900—2,196; 1970—741
6. Architectural points of interest: Main street commercial structures; Beaumont Hotel; Western Hotel; opera house (Wrights Hall); Elks Club; Ouray County Courthouse; fine Victorian houses.

RICO

1. Dolores County
2. State Road 145
3. 8,900 ft.
4. Founded: Late 1870s
5. Population: 1890—1,134; 1900—811; 1970—275
6. Architectural points of interest: Dolores County Courthouse

ROLLINSVILLE

1. Gilpin County
2. State Road 119
3. 8,200 ft.
4. Founding date unknown
5. Population: 1900—231

RUSSELL GULCH

1. Gilpin County
2. State Road 279
3. 9,500 ft.
4. Founded: Late 1850s

5. Population: 1860—480; 1880—543; 1890—673
6. Architectural points of interest: Fine stonework in walls constructed by Cornish stonemasons

SALINA

1. Boulder County
2. Four Mile Canyon Road
3. 6,500 ft.
4. Founded: Mid 1870s
5. Population: 1900—462

SILVER CLIFF

1. Custer County
2. State Road 96
3. 8,000 ft.
4. Founded: Late 1870s
5. Population: 1880—5,040; 1890—546; 1900—576; 1970—126
6. Architectural points of interest: City Hall and Fire Company

SILVER PLUME

1. Clear Creek County
2. Interstate 70
3. 9,175 ft.
4. Founded: Early 1870s
5. Population: 1890—908; 1900—775; 1960—86
6. Architectural points of interest: Main street commercial structures; jail; bandstand

SILVERTON

1. San Juan County
2. U.S. 550 and State Road 110
3. 9,302 ft.
4. Founded: Mid 1870s
5. Population: 1890—1,154; 1900—1,360; 1970—797
6. Architectural points of interest: Entire town offers fine examples of residential, commercial, institutional, and industrial buildings including San Juan County Courthouse; jail; Grande Imperial Hotel; main street commercial structures; fine Victorian houses.

ST. ELMO AND ROMLEY

1. Chaffee County
2. State Road 162
3. Altitude not available
4. Founded: Late 1870s
5. Population: 1900—64
6. Architectural points of interest: City Hall and Fire Company; schoolhouse; log houses; main street commercial structures; mining and milling remains

TELLURIDE AND PANDORA

1. San Miguel County

2. State Road 145
3. 8,500 ft.
4. Founded: Late 1870s
5. Population: 1890—766; 1900—2,446; 1970—553
6. Architectural points of interest: Main street commercial buildings; San Miguel County Courthouse; Sheridan Hotel; Pick and Gad sporting house; railroad station; some fine Victorian houses

VICTOR

1. Teller County
2. State Road 67
3. 9,900 ft.
4. Founded: Early 1890s
5. Population: 1900—4,986; 1970—258
6. Architectural points of interest: Entire town offers fine examples of residential, commercial, institutional, and industrial buildings including main street commercial structures; City Hall and Fire Station; churches; Masonic Hall; Gold Coin Club; mining and milling remains.

WESTCLIFFE

1. Custer County
2. State Roads 96 and 69
3. 7,800 ft.
4. Founded: Mid 1880s
5. Population: 1890—192; 1900—256; 1970—243

Notes

Chapter 1

1. Frank Fossett, *Colorado* (New York: C. G. Crawford, 1880), p. 120.
2. Quoted in LeRoy R. Hafen, *Colorado* (Denver: Peerless Publishing Co., 1933), p. 147.

Chapter 2

1. Quoted in LeRoy R. Hafen, *Colorado* (Denver: Peerless Publishing Co., 1933), pp. 202–3.
2. Muriel S. Wolle, *Stampede to Timberline* (Boulder, Colo.: Muriel S. Wolle, 1949), p. 321.
3. Duane A. Smith, *Rocky Mountain Mining Camps* (Bloomington: Indiana University Press, 1967), pp. 4–5.
4. Caroline Bancroft, *Historic Central City* (Boulder, Colo.: Johnson Publishing Co., 1957), p. 16.
5. Leland Feitz, *A Quick History of Creede, Colorado Boom Town* (Denver: Golden Bell Press, 1969), p. 24.
6. Smith, *Rocky Mountain Mining Camps,* p. 9.

Chapter 3

1. John Maass, *The Gingerbread Age* (New York: Rinehart & Co., 1957), p. 14.
2. Sandra Dallas, *Cherry Creek Gothic* (Norman: University of Oklahoma Press, 1971), p. 21.
3. Bainbridge Bunting, *Houses of Boston's Back Bay* (Cambridge, Mass.: Harvard University Press, Belknap Press, 1967), p. 212.

Chapter 4

1. William H. Larimer, quoted in Sandra Dallas, *Cherry Creek Gothic* (Norman: University of Oklahoma Press, 1971), p. 5.
2. Quoted in LeRoy R. Hafen, *Colorado* (Denver: Peerless Publishing Co., 1933), p. 145.
3. Bainbridge Bunting, *Houses of Boston's Back Bay* (Cambridge, Mass.: Harvard University Press, Belknap Press, 1967), p. 230.
4. Ibid., p. 333.

Chapter 5

1. Quoted in Muriel S. Wolle, *Stampede to Timberline* (Boulder, Colo.: Muriel S. Wolle, 1949), p. 291.

2. Quoted in Wolle, *Stampede*, p. 216.

3. Wolle, *Stampede*, p. 324.

4. Robert L. Brown, *An Empire of Silver* (Caldwell, Idaho: Caxton Printers, 1965), p. 205.

5. Quoted in LeRoy R. Hafen, *Colorado* (Denver: Peerless Publishing Co., 1933), p. 146.

6. Bainbridge Bunting, *Houses of Boston's Back Bay* (Cambridge, Mass.: Harvard University Press, Belknap Press, 1967), p. 188.

7. Smith, *Rocky Mountain Mining Camps*, p. 69.

8. Lucius Beebe, *Highball* (New York: D. Appleton-Century Co., 1945), p. 163.

9. Ibid., p. 138.

10. Quoted in Leland Feitz, *A Quick History of Creede, Colorado Boom Town* (Denver: Golden Bell Press, 1969), p. 35.

11. Wolle, *Stampede*, p. 45.

12. Quoted in Gilbert A. Lathrop, *Little Engines and Big Men* (Caldwell, Idaho: Caxton Printers, 1955), p. 30.

13. Henry Villard, quoted in Hafen, *Colorado*, p. 145.

14. *Hotel de Paris* (Georgetown, Colo.: Museum of the National Society of Colonial Dames of America in the State of Colorado), p. 4.

15. Wolle, *Stampede*, p. 14.

16. Ibid., p. 48.

17. Quoted in Sandra Dallas, *Cherry Creek Gothic* (Norman: University of Oklahoma Press, 1971), p. 230.

18. Quoted in Hafen, *Colorado*, p. 149.

Chapter 6

1. Robert L. Brown, *An Empire of Silver* (Caldwell, Idaho: Caxton Printers, 1965), p. 111.

2. *Georgetown: A Walking Tour Guide* (Georgetown, Colo.: Georgetown Historical Society, 1973), p. 16.

3. Quoted in *St. Patrick's Church 1896-1971, Seventy-Fifth Anniversary* (Telluride, Colo.), p. 4.

4. Duane A. Smith, *Rocky Mountain Mining Camps* (Bloomington: Indiana University Press, 1967), p. 119.

Chapter 7

1. Frank Fossett, *Colorado* (New York: C. G. Crawford, 1880), p. 129.

2. Muriel S. Wolle, *Stampede to Timberline* (Boulder, Colo.: Muriel S. Wolle, 1949), p. 52.

3. Perry Eberhart, *Guide to the Colorado Ghost Towns and Mining Camps* (Chicago: Swallow Press, Sage Books, 1969), p. 63.

4. See Wolle, *Stampede*, p. 179.

5. Caroline Bancroft, *Unique Ghost Towns and Mountain Spots* (Boulder, Colo.: Johnson Publishing Co., 1967), p. 34.

6. Otis E. Young, Jr., *Western Mining* (Norman: University of Oklahoma Press, 1970), p. 153.

7. Fossett, *Colorado*, p. 452.

8. Ibid., p. 236.

9. Leland Feitz, *A Quick History of Creede, Colorado Boom Town* (Denver: Golden Bell Press, 1969), p. 25.

Selected Bibliography

Bancroft, Caroline. *Historic Central City.* Boulder, Colo.: Johnson Publishing Co., 1957.

————. *Unique Ghost Towns and Mountain Spots.* Boulder, Colo.: Johnson Publishing Co., 1967.

Beebe, Lucius. *Highball: A Pageant of Trains.* New York: D. Appleton-Century Co., 1945.

Bernhordi, Robert. *The Buildings of Berkeley.* Berkeley, Calif.: Lederer Street and Zeus Co., 1971.

Brown, Robert L. *An Empire of Silver: A History of the San Juan Silver Rush.* Caldwell, Idaho: Caxton Printers, 1965.

Bunting, Bainbridge. *Houses of Boston's Back Bay.* Cambridge, Mass.: Harvard University Press, Belknap Press, 1967.

Burnham, Alan. *New York Landmarks.* Middletown, Conn.: Wesleyan University Press, Municipal Art Society of New York, 1963.

Campen, Richard N. *Architecture of the Western Reserve.* Cleveland: Press of Case Western Reserve University, 1971.

Dallas, Sandra. *Cherry Creek Gothic.* Norman: University of Oklahoma Press, 1971.

————. *Gaslights and Gingerbread.* Denver: Sage Books, 1965.

Eberhart, Perry. *Guide to the Colorado Ghost Towns and Mining Camps.* Chicago: Swallow Press, Sage Books, 1969.

Facts on San Miguel County and Telluride, Colorado. Telluride: San Miguel Historical Society, n.d.

Feitz, Leland. *A Quick History of Creede, Colorado Boom Town.* Denver: Golden Bell Press, 1969.

————. *A Quick History of Victor.* Colorado Springs, Colo.: Graphic Services Printer, 1969.

————. *Myers Avenue: A Quick History of Cripple Creek's Red-Light District.* Denver: Golden Bell Press, 1967.

Fossett, Frank. *Colorado.* New York: C. G. Crawford, Printer, 1880.

Georgetown: A Walking Tour Guide. Georgetown, Colo.: Georgetown Historical Society, 1973.

Hafen, LeRoy R. *Colorado: The Story of a Western Commonwealth.* Denver: Peerless Publishing Co., 1933.

Helmers, Dow. "W. S. Stratton and the Bowl of Gold." *Empire Magazine, Denver Post,* September 16, 1973, pp. 68–69.

Henderson, Junius. *Colorado: Short Studies of Its Past and Present.* Boulder: University of Colorado Press, 1927.

Hotel de Paris. Georgetown, Colo.: Museum of the National Society of Colonial Dames of America in the State of Colorado, n.d.

Idaho Springs, Colorado. Idaho Springs Chamber of Commerce, n.d.

Ingham, G. Thomas. *Digging Gold among the Rockies.* Philadelphia: Hubbard Brothers, 1882.

Jarvis, Marion. *The Strater Story.* Durango, Colo.: Durango Herald Printing, 1969.

Lathrop, Gilbert A. *Little Engines and Big Men.* Caldwell, Idaho: Caxton Printers, 1955.

Maass, John. *The Gingerbread Age.* New York: Rinehart & Co., 1957.

————. *The Victorian Home in America.* New York: Hawthorn Books, 1972.

Marshall, Thomas Maitland. *Early Records of Gilpin, Colorado, 1859–1861.* Boulder, Colo., 1920.

Mazzulla, Fred M. *The First 100 Years: Cripple Creek and the Pike's Peak Region.* Denver: A. B. Hirschfield Press, 1964.

Meeks, Carroll L. V. *The Railroad Station: An Architectural History.* New Haven, Conn.: Yale University Press, 1956.

St. Patrick's Church 1896–1971, Seventy-Fifth Anniversary. Telluride, Colo.

Scully, Vincent, Jr. *The Shingle Style.* New Haven, Conn.: Yale University Press, 1955.

Sloan, Samuel, compiler. *The Architectural Review and American Builders' Journal* I (1869).

Smith, Duane A. *Rocky Mountain Mining Camps: The Urban Frontier.* Bloomington: Indiana University Press, 1967.

The Pioneer Trail through Historic Boulder. Boulder, Colo.: Pioneer Museum, Boulder Historical Society, n.d.

"The Short Line" Gold Camp Road Auto Tour. U.S. Department of Agriculture, Forest Service.

Voss, Walter C., and Henry, Ralph Coolidge. *Architectural Construction.* Vol. I. New York: John Wiley and Sons, 1925.

Watkins, T. H. *Gold and Silver in the West.* Palo Alto, Calif.: American West Publishing Co., 1971.

Weslager, C. A. *The Log Cabin in America: From Pioneer Days to the Present.* New Brunswick, N.J.: Rutgers University Press, 1969.

Williams, Henry Lionell, and Williams, Ottalie K. *A Guide to Old American Houses, 1700–1900.* New York: A. S. Barnes and Co., 1962.

Wolle, Muriel S. *Stampede to Timberline.* Boulder, Colo.: Muriel S. Wolle, 1949.

Workers of the Writers' Program of the Work Projects Administration in the State of Colorado. *Colorado: A Guide to the Highest State.* New York: Hastings House, 1941.

Young, Otis E., Jr. *Western Mining.* Norman: University of Oklahoma Press, 1970.

Index